I0559154

Looming
Beads & Fibers

Ann Benson

For
Linnea Benson McGurk
Eric Robert Benson
and Carl Edward Benson II

Ann Benson Publishing
Port Orange Florida/South Dennis Massachusetts

ISBN 9798326905260

ann benson
publishing

Contents

I have the immense privilege

of floating through many different craft worlds, among them beading, weaving and the needle arts. This book is an intersection of those worlds, the natural outgrowth of bringing together the things that surround me in my studio every day.

The projects in this book are more accurately referred to as **tapestry** rather than weaving. All of the projects are done with needles carrying fibers or beads. The work is done on a tabletop, hand-held, or lap loom.

True weaving is largely done with shuttles carrying the thread on a standing loom with one or more heddles, and has a markedly different set of rules and recommendations. The "weaving" done in the designs herein is really a form of tapestry and/or embroidery.

No matter what we call the lovely process in which we're about to engage, **beneath all is the loom.**

Looms vary tremendously in size, functionality and, most notably, price. If you're able to afford a multi-function loom, you'll probably be able to use it for almost any small tapestry project with a few exceptions.

I've worked on a Mirrix loom for larger projects and wrap-around warp projects for many years and I could not love it more than I do. But if this type of loom is not for you, you can make your own very functional loom using widely available materials. It may surprise you just how easy it is.

Warping instructions will vary from loom to loom; in almost all cases, the manufacturer of a loom will include specific directions for assembly and warping.

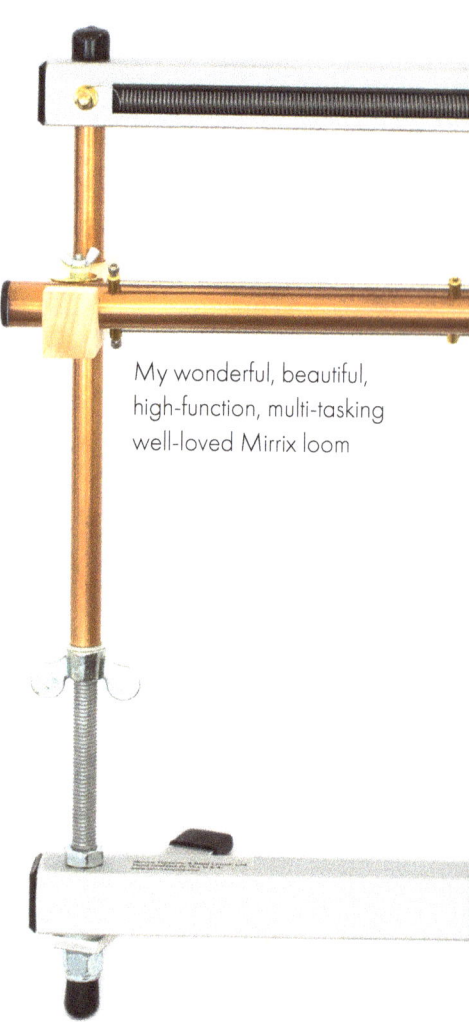

My wonderful, beautiful, high-function, multi-tasking well-loved Mirrix loom

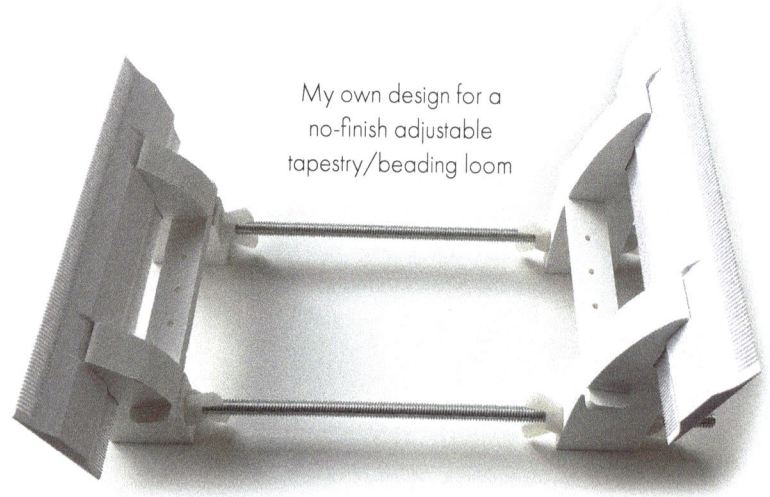

My own design for a no-finish adjustable tapestry/beading loom

Making your own no-finish loom

The materials required to create a highly functional no-finish loom are easily obtained in hardware stores, supermarkets, lumber yards and on-line outlets.

Here's what you will need to make the loom's base:
Two wood pieces cut to 2.5" high x 8" wide x .5" (minimum)
Two 12" lengths of fully threaded steel rod 5/16" diameter, 18 threads per inch (1/4" rod will warp)
Six 5/16-18 wing nuts and two 5/16-18 plain nuts (nylon preferred over metal)

Here's what you will need to create warp prongs:
Two ordinary hair combs with consistently spaced teeth and a wide enough base to drill
Four small wood screws
OR a lot of size 17 x 1" wire brads

Using a 3/8" drill bit, make four holes in the wood so the center of the holes is 1" above the bottom edge of the wood.

To use brads as prongs, mark the top edge of the wood at equal intervals, 4mm recommended. Carefully hammer the brads on the marks. You may find it helpful to use a plier to hold the brads as you hammer, both for the sake of your fingers and for placement accuracy.

To use a comb as prongs: Drill two holes through each comb base with a drill size appropriate to the size of the wood screws. Mark dots on the wood for placement and drill short holes (not all the way through). Secure the combs to the outside of the wood panel with the screws. Because the combs/brads are not slanted, you will need masking tape as you warp to prevent slippage.

THE WING NUTS ON BOTH SIDES OF THIS WOOD BASE ARE ADJUSTED OUTWARD OR INWARD FOR SIZE, OUTWARD FOR TENSIONING WARP

THESE TWO WING NUTS REMAIN STATIONARY

HEX NUTS REMAIN STATIONARY

This little **no-finish "loom"** was made using **20-gauge clear plastic**, about the weight of that excessive plastic packaging we all despise. I used Grafix 20-gauge plastic sheeting, but a plastic milk carton would also be an appropriate weight to use if you don't have 20-gauge plastic laying around. I printed my design in color on paper/label stock first, with the warp separations at printed both ends. The paper is adhered to the plastic surface. **Warp slots are cut** prior to adding the STRONG warp (cut plastic can have abrasive edges) which is run back and forth between slots, so there are only two warp ends to finish.

IMPORTANT: On any no-finish loom, the top and bottom edges must both have two rows of plain tabby over one warp to secure the edges, or a row of beading that includes all the warps. Thereafter the weave can be worked over multiple warps.

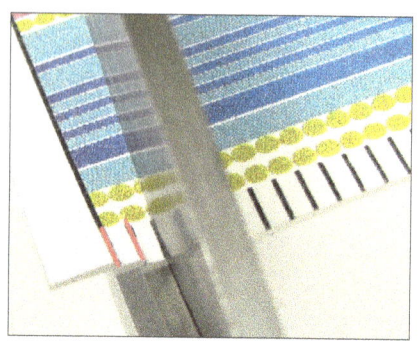

After **knotting the warp thread**, the warp is run back and forth between the ends, through the slots. The warp tension will force a curve. Though this photo does not show tape on the ends, it's a VERY good idea to **use masking tape over the slotted ends** to keep the warp in place. **End with another knot.** Force a slight curve as you add warps; you can adjust tension of each warp span individually after all the warps are in place.

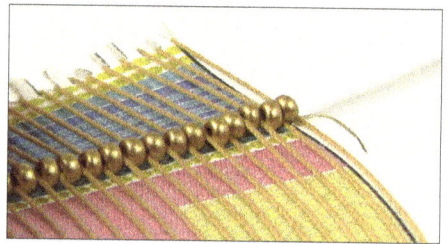

Because this loom is flexible, you'll be able to bend it as needed to push needles through beads (another good reason to tape the ends!). **This type of loom should have an even number or warps** yielding an odd number of spaces between warps.

Strong cardboard can be made into a loom with just a pair of scissors. This one features a raised bridge that separates the warp from the main cardboard sheet. This type of loom is better for projects using larger beads such as 6⁰s and heavier fibers like bulky knitting yarn. This kind of loom is great for kids and is extremely portable.

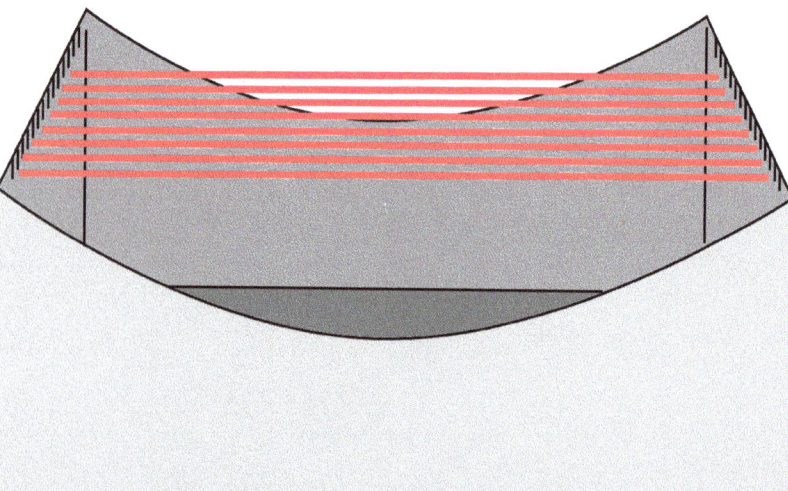

The venerable shoe box loom. Choose a sturdy box for this! Cut curves in the long sides and slots in the short ends. This is great for quick chunky projects using heavier or thicker fibers.

Basic Tapestry Weaves

The basic techniques of adding fibers to a small woven piece are so similar to embroidery that they might as well be called stitches. In true weaving the thread is generally passed through the warps using a shuttle in a repeating pattern that yields a fabric with a specific appearance. **In tapestry, we are instead using a needle to carry thread/fiber** and incorporate it into the warp, and while we are creating a fabric of sorts, the difference in scale is truly definitive.

Plain tabby

In **plain tabby weave,** the most basic stitch, threads are passed over one warp and under the next across the row. In the following row, the thread is passed over and under again, but the OVERS and UNDERS alternate from the previous row. When the rows are compressed, a neat, tight weave results.

Plain tabby can be worked over multiple warps to adds texture and interest to your project. **On a no-finish loom, it's essential to weave two rows of tabby on single warps on both outer ends** of your weave; you can use a fine thread that disappears under heavier threads. This will stabilize the ends of the weave on removal from the loom.

Plain tabby worked over two warps with a ribbon-type thread, loosely compressed, and plain tabby worked over a single warp, tightly compressed.

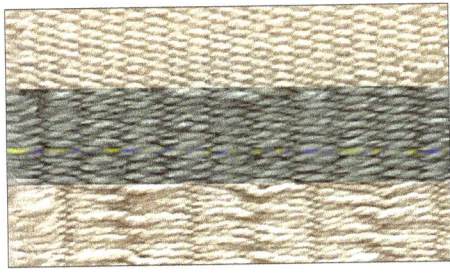

Plain tabby in 8/2 tencel worked over one warp (top), two warps(center) and three warps (bottom).

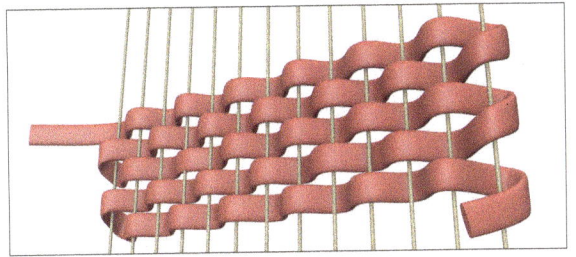

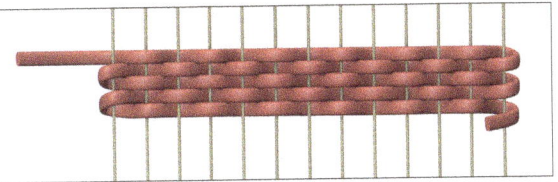

Plain tabby weave over a single warp with a single ply of thread, loose and uncompressed (angled view, upper), and plain tabby compressed to form a "fabric" (flat view, lower).

Beads sit between the warps while fiber sits over and under the warps. When weaving beads and fibers in adjacent sections, the edges of the bead sections will be slightly recessed.

Pick and pick

In this variation of tabby **two colors are woven in alternating rows so rows of the same colors are aligned in their over-under positions.** The result is a series of vertical "lines" when compressed. This stitch can be worked over a single warp for narrow lines or multiple warps for fatter lines. It's a distinctive weave that is popular and iconic.

Pick and pick over one warp using a doubled strand of fine Fleur de Paris wool

Pick and pick over two using 10/2 tencel doubled, with four starting and ending rows in one color

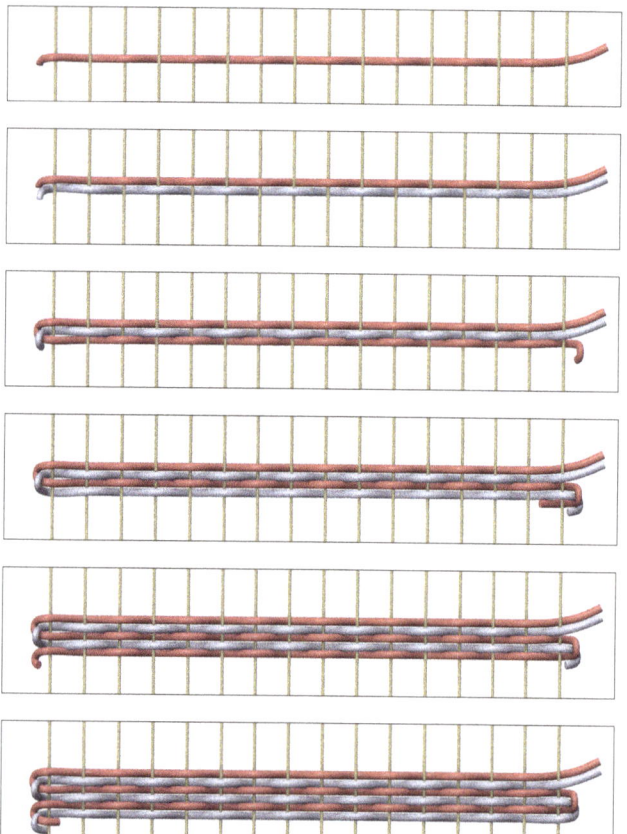

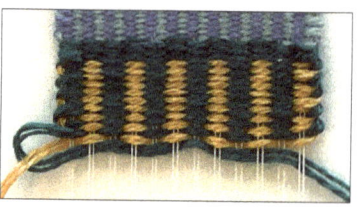

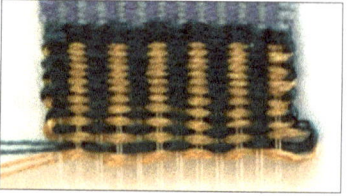

Thread passes are made in alternating colors as shown in the progression at left. Threads are looped around each other at the end-of-row turns (both sides) to stabilize the weave. The example above shows the method when working over TWO warps; the progression at left shows the stitch worked over ONE warp. The end turns will be different based on the number of warps you are passing over, but in all cases the ends are looped.

Pick and Pick can be worked over more than two warps; the upper diagram below shows the weave over FOUR warps. Moreover, your weave does not need to be symmetrical or even, as shown in the lower diagram below. You can alter the spacing of the overs and unders to create varied vertical ridges. These diagrams do not show the end-of-row turns but turns would be made in the same manner as in the realistic diagrams.

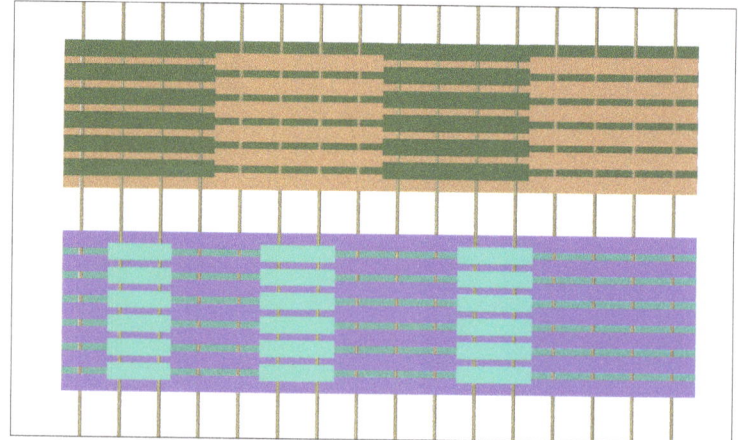

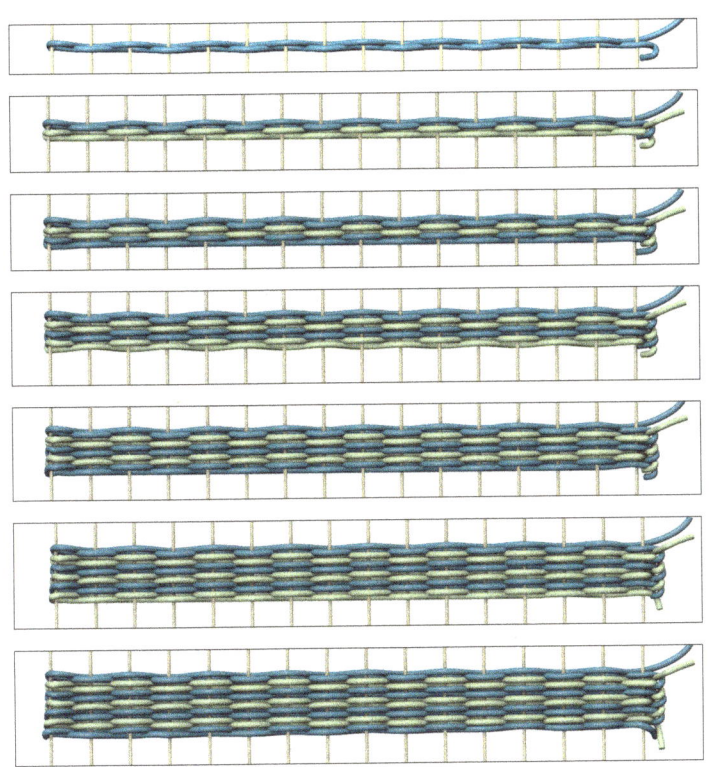

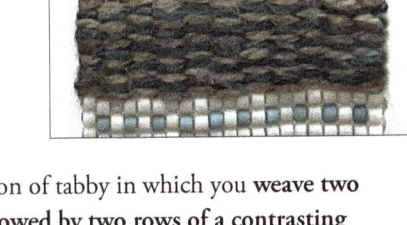

Wave stitch

This is a subtle variation of tabby in which you **weave two rows of one color followed by two rows of a contrasting color.** When tightly compressed the colors form a slightly wavy line. This technique can be used in places where you want a fairly tight fiber weave but a bit more visual interest than plain tabby in all one color. You can experiment with different textures of fiber (one matte, one silky or metallic) in the same color.

The progression of chain stitch, step by step

Chain stitch

This embroidery technique is **best used as a decoration over existing woven areas,** and as a visual separator or outline. The weight of your fiber and the size of each stitch will dramatically alter the appearance. Fine fiber single-ply yields a thin, subtle outline; heavy or multiple fibers over more than one warp have a distinctive embroidery appearance.

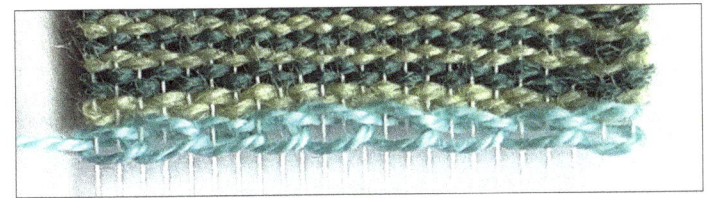

Soumak weave

This is another basic stitch, **an excellent choice when you want some textu**re. Because of its thickness, this diagonally angled stitch is easy to start and end threads; there's plenty of room for burying and trimming threads both on front and back.

In this example we're showing the stitch worked over two threads. Loop your starting end around the outermost warp to secure it (you'll bury it within the weave itself later) then scoop forward under two warps, then stitch backward over a smaller number of warps. The over-then-under ratio can be changed, resulting in a different appearance. The stitch-motion is the **rough equivalent of the outline stitch** in hand embroidery, though there is more texture in soumak.

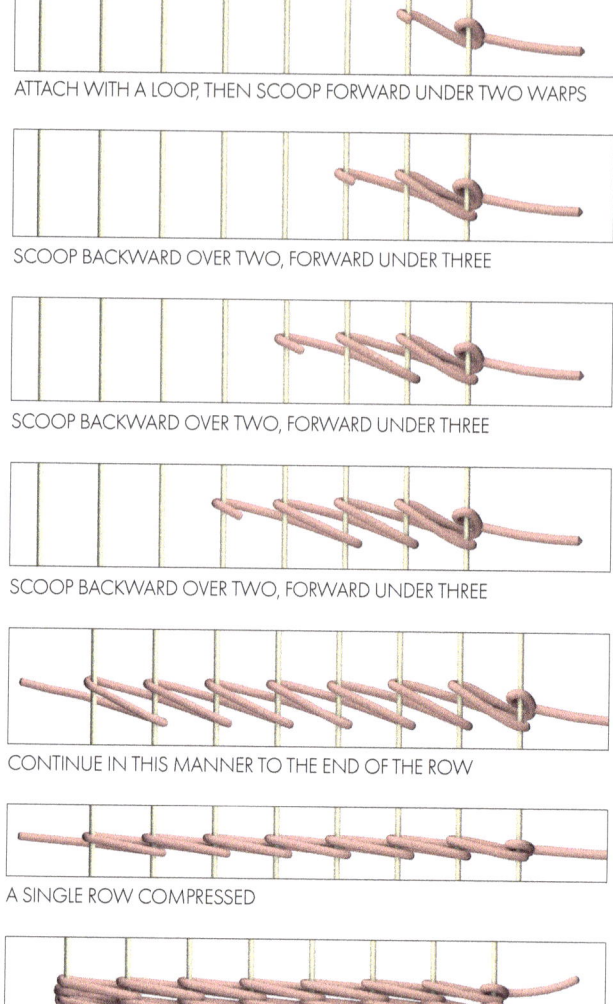

ATTACH WITH A LOOP, THEN SCOOP FORWARD UNDER TWO WARPS

SCOOP BACKWARD OVER TWO, FORWARD UNDER THREE

SCOOP BACKWARD OVER TWO, FORWARD UNDER THREE

SCOOP BACKWARD OVER TWO, FORWARD UNDER THREE

CONTINUE IN THIS MANNER TO THE END OF THE ROW

A SINGLE ROW COMPRESSED

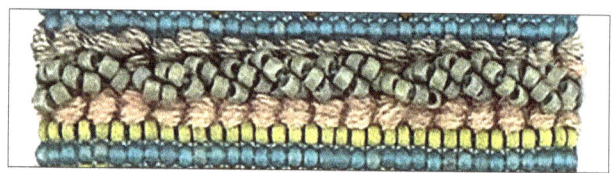

A SECOND ROW ADDED (OPPOSITE DIRECTION) AND COMPRESSED

An interesting effect happens when you alternate the direction of adjacent rows of soumak weave

Soumak can be padded by running a thread back through the upper stitches of a row. Here the padding is done on the upper and lower limits of a section with multiple rows of plain tabby between, decorated with bugle beads.

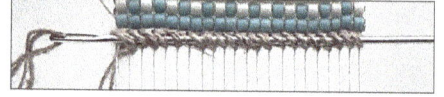

When soumak is worked over-one/under-two, **a beaded appearance emerges.** At right the fiber section has three separate rows of soumak. The top and bottom rows are worked over-one/under-two. The center section is worked in cylinder beads with the "over" part of the stitch comprised of four beads and the "under" part a naked beading thread.

Encroaching soumak

This stitch gives a **padded appearance** with no visible warps. Threads are scooped forward under the warp and then stitched backwards over the warp with the needle piercing both the over and under stitch thread (but never the warp threads). This stitch is best worked between rows of beads or plain tabby in fiber. It has a chain-like (and slightly messy) appearance, and is very strong. Be careful with your tension in this stitch; it's easy to tighten it too much, but hard to rip and redo if it narrows. The rose band is worked two-over/four under; the teal band is four-over/six-under.

Starting a new fiber

If you are using a **doubled thread, simply loop it around a warp** then even the ends before putting the fiber onto a needle. When using a **single ply,** you'll have a thread tail that will need to be woven in, so **always leave a tail that is long enough to secure later.** If it's too short to put it easily onto a needle, it will be difficult to secure it.

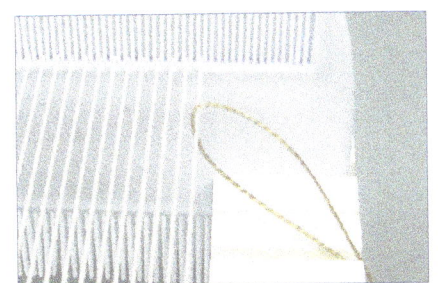

Starting a doubled thread by looping around the outer warp

Securing fiber tails

Thread tails can be secured within the weave; if you've been weaving with a blunt-pointed needle, switch to a sharp-pointed needle which will pass through your weave with less disruption of the weave.

With a doubled thread, secure the two thread ends separately, in opposite directions if possible.

You can also catch the tail of a new thread within the edges of the weave until it is secure. Be sure to secure the ending tail of that thread in the opposite edge of the weave to avoid a lumpy appearance.

ABOVE: Using a sharp needle to weave the thread tail into the existing weave.

LEFT: catching the starting tail of a new thread within the outer edge of the warp as you weave

Starting/ending beading threads

Use a simple knot to secure the beading thread to an outer or inner warp. Leave a tail long enough to secure later.

To secure a nylon thread, run it through existing beads, reversing direction a couple of times for security. Trim carefully to avoid cutting warp threads.

BELOW: Attach a new beading nylon thread with a simple knot

BELOW: Weaving nylon thread tails into the beads

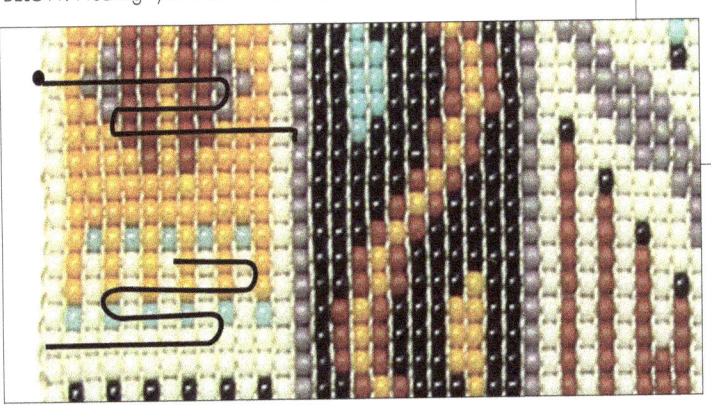

Weaving seed beads in rows

Seed bead rows can be worked into looming/weaving designs in different methods, depending on the look you want.

Beads of any size can be woven but sizes larger than 8° in densely beaded designs will be heavy and might require substantial backing to retain their woven shape. The sizes shown here are good choices for weaving beads in rows in smaller projects.

Finer warps will be less visible in the final weave. Heavier warps will create a wider weave and will be visible (you may like this look!). You can incorporate visible warp as part of your design.

BEAD IMAGES ARE LARGER THAN ACTUAL SIZE

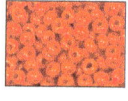

Czech 11°s (2 x 1 mm) are more oval/elliptical in shape than Japanese, and can be slightly smaller.

Japanese 11°s (2.1 x 1.1 mm) have larger holes than Czech and their edges are generally more squared.

11° seed beads are only minutely wider than cylinder beads, having seventeen (17) beads per horizontal woven inch, but are slightly longer, having twelve (12) rows in the vertical inch. Seed beads are in the 3D geometric shape known as "torus" in shape (imagine a donut or tire) with smaller holes than cylinder beads. I often mix Czech and Japanese seed beads in one project (above), even though they can be minutely different in size and shape. Purists may want to stick to one country of origin, but I like an imperfect look. Warp and weft can both be size D beading nylon (above), or you can warp with beading micro cord.

Japanese cylinder beads (1.6 x 1.5 mm) (Delicas, Aikos/Treasures). Size 11 is most used, but they are also available in size 15 (1.3 x 1 mm) and larger sizes. Large holes, a dream to weave.

Size 11 cylinder beads (Miyuki Delicas, Toho Aikos, Toho Treasures) are often used for fully-beaded designs. The **best warps for cylinders are beading nylon D and beading micro cord** (appropriate for very fine macrame). The number of beads in a horizontal inch (including warps) is 17.5, and the number of vertical rows per inch is fifteen (15). Beading nylon D will fit easily within their large holes.

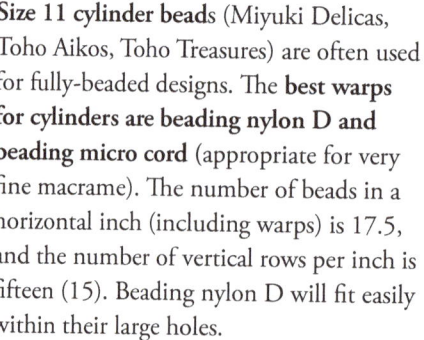

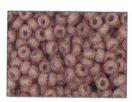

Japanese 15°s (1.3 x 1.5 mm) Miyuki and Toho are the same size, Matsunos tend to be a bit larger. Size 12 needles can work, but have a size 13 on hand.

15° seed beads (Japanese) are likely the smallest size you'll weave; there are twenty (20) beads per inch of horizontal row and 15.5 rows per vertical inch of weave. They are much narrower than cylinders but almost the same length. Use size D beading nylon/beading micro cord for warp, and size B or D beading nylon for securing the beads. **Czech 13° seed beads** are about the same size and can be mixed with Japanese 15°s.

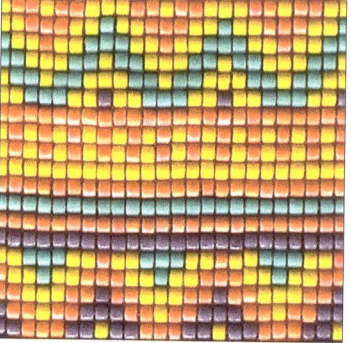

A solid pattern of bead looming is made by securing beads between warps with two passes of thread: one pass below the warp and one pass over the warp. The warp and securing thread will be slightly visible in the spaces between warps. The number of warps will always be one more than the number of beads in the horizontal rows of your pattern. An even number of warps will yield an odd number of beads in the horizontal row, as an odd number of warps will yield an even number of beads in the horizontal row.

IF YOU LEARN ONLY ONE THING FROM THIS BOOK, LEARN THIS:

BE CAREFUL NOT TO PIERCE THE WARP THREAD WITH YOUR WEAVING NEEDLE. IF YOU DO, YOUR WEAVE MAY NOT SUCCEED.

ABOVE: The weft securing thread has pierced the warp thread and the weave cannot be adjusted. If this happens, the best solution is to remove rows until you reach the piercing point and redo the rows without piercing the warp.

The **starting tail** of a bead section should be secured in the rows AFTER the attachment point, and the **end tails** should be secured in the rows BEFORE the ending point to minimize thread bulk within the bead holes. Note that if you don't mind weaving with thread ends unsecured, those ends can later be used for finishing and decoration when the weave is complete.

STARTING WEFT TAIL

ENDING WEFT TAIL

Tie your thread onto the outermost warp on the side of your non-dominant hand. Pick up the beads of the row in order from left to right (if right-handed) or right to left (if left-handed). Align the beads between the warps and push them upward.

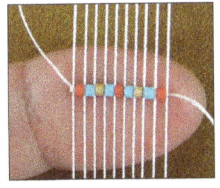

OVERHEAD VIEW

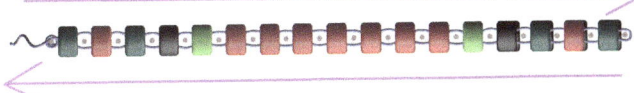

Run the needle back through the beads of the first row, OVER the warp thread. Take care not to pierce the warp threads with your needle. You may need to move the weave on the warps, and if the weft has been run through the warp thread, you will not be able to do so. Take the slack out of the thread so there is little or no space between the warp threads and the beads without puckering; the width should be consistent from start to end of the weave. This completes the first row.

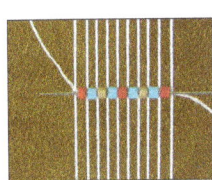

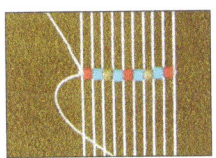

Simple knot tie-on

Threads looped from front to back to start each new row

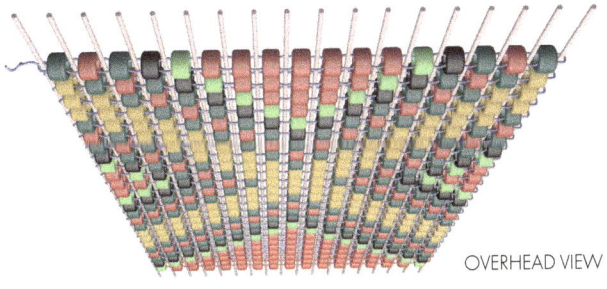

OVERHEAD VIEW

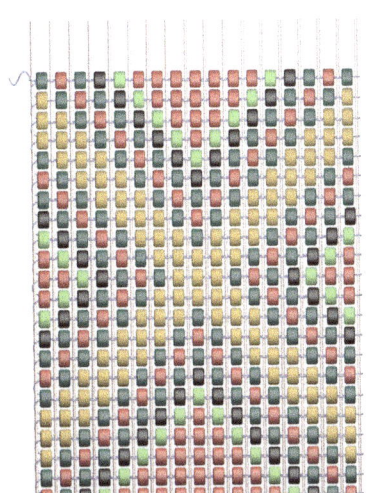

FRONT VIEW

In this image, the full weave of a symmetrical design is shown, with seventeen beads woven between eighteen warps, with the design mirrored at the vertical center.

Weaving beads directly into fiber sections

In these **overview** examples, beads and fibers are shown being worked together using multiple different methods. **Details** will be given within the specific directions for projects.

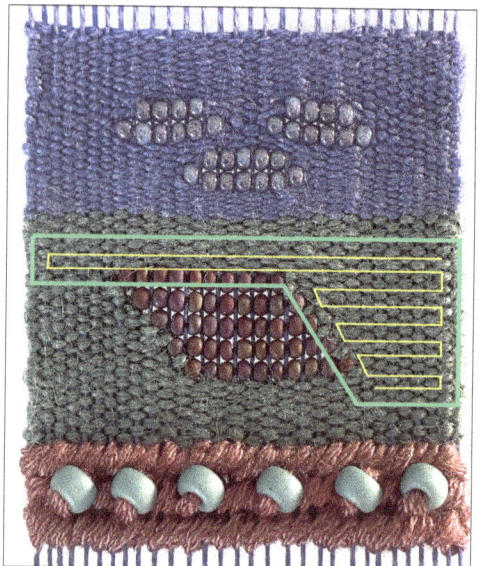

This section is begun with basic tabby using lace-weight thread on cotton warp of the same color. In the three Japanese 11° motifs the row is started in tabby, then beads are picked up UNDERNEATH the warps. The spaces needed for the beads are skipped and the tabby weave is taken up again until the next beaded section. This method requires a fine weaving fiber so the needle can fit through the bead holes.

When the weave goes in the opposite direction, it passes through the beads OVER the warps. In this center section Czech 11°s are woven into the warp with nylon thread before the wool fibers are added around them. The full width is woven in fiber for several rows then worked beside the beads as shown in the exaggerated lined area. The initial fiber is secured, then a new fiber is added at the top row of the beaded section. The weave continues to the bottom of the beaded section, then in the full width until the section is complete. In this lower section the initial fiber row is woven in soumak.

In the second row, Japanese 6°s are picked up with the needle as part of the weaving stitch and secured to the row as it is woven. This gives a slightly different look than adding the beads with lighter thread after the weave is complete; the beads are forced into a diagonal position for an interesting effect. The third row is woven in soumak without beads.

Weaving beads adjacent to fiber sections

In this crazy bead-fiber combo you can see how beads and fibers intersect in direct contact. Here the top section is woven fully in tabby using lace-weight teal wool. The bead rows were then added on the left. The sock-weight lavender yarn is woven in and compressed to about three weave rows per bead row. Both fiber and bead rows are looped into the same warp so one is shared by both beads and fibers.

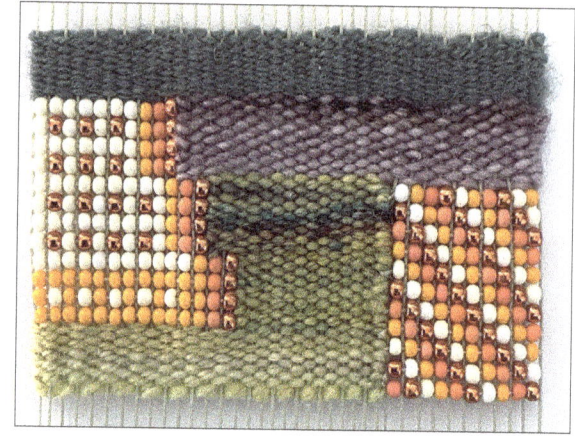

After the lavender section the olive variegated section (fingering-weight wool), was woven in tabby. The right-most bead section was added after the olive section was fully complete, including the lowest portion where the weave goes out to the left edge. Because the fibers and beading nylon threads were looped into their adjacent sections, this weave is substantial and has no visible gaps. It is strong and will likely retain its shape with minimal or no backing.

Below: Doubled 10/2 cotton fiber is secured to the warp in which the beading thread is started and ended. Note how the fiber encroaches the beads; as the weave is compressed, the fiber area becomes a solid "fabric."

Left: A good example of weaving adjacent sections of fiber and beads. Fibers are worked into the last warp of each beaded area, except in the buttonhole, in which the fibers are worked over half the warps, and the half-sections remain disconnected so the button will fit through the opening. Note the three beaded rows at the outside of the buttonhole area; they form an attractive border at the end of the bracelet. No beaded rows are required at the other end as it is tucked under.

Embellishing with beads

If you've ever done bead embroidery on a fabric or non-woven surface, you'll recognize these techniques.

You can add surface beads to a design that is woven fully in fibers, fully woven in beads, or woven in a combination of both. The techniques are much the same, with only slight variations.

You'll need a working thread, obviously; this will almost always be a nylon beading thread. If your design has fully or partially beaded areas you can use a leftover thread tail from the bead weaving to secure the embellishments. Doing this mitigates the need to secure the thread within the weave. I often tape or pin a nylon beading thread tail to the loom or a completed section of the weave to keep that thread out of the way but preserve it for later use in embellishment.

But if you don't have an already existing thread to use, secure an appropriate length of nylon beading thread to the outermost warp as you would if you were going to weave full rows of beads, leaving just enough excess to bury later. If you're adding a backing to your piece as part of the finishing process, it's not necessary to keep your weave-back neat, though this is a good practice in general. But a mess isn't a mess if no one sees it!

This design is first woven entirely in fiber, then embellished with beads on the surface and edges

Decorations are added over both beaded sections and fiber sections in this necklace. The dotting of gold beads on the outer edge of each narrow panel is a consolidating design factor

In this doodled design, decorative beads are added after the weave is fully complete. The weave itself contains several sections of beading. **Drops and fringes are added** so that fully beaded strands hang over the woven sections.

It was something of a challenge to keep the beading thread invisible in this piece. That was especially true in the edges where decorative beads were added to create a sense of alignment with the painted non-woven strips.

Adding beads to a fully-fibered design

In this *Chroma* design, a variety of weaving techniques and fibers are used in the woven strip, which is worked on a warp of size D beading nylon in cotton, tencel, silk and other bulkier fibers. **All of the fiber ends are secured on the reverse** by weaving in, often with a with small swipes of glue on the end thread.

Shown below are examples of the standard methods for securing beads of different shapes to surfaces, in this case, a hand woven "fabric." **To secure a beading thread in a fiber section**, run it invisibly back and forth within the fiber weave until it's secure. A buttonhole closure is used with three amethyst rounds as buttons, each secured with one 15° bead, so that area remains undecorated.

Use a single or doubled thread to secure beads, depending on the surface of the bead. Cut beads like bugles and crystals have sharp edges, and should be sewn in place with a doubled thread or two separate passes. To secure a finished thread, run it back and forth as invisibly as possible within a fiber section and trim, taking GREAT care not to cut working threads.

Adding fibers to a fully beaded design

What you can do is somewhat limited by the naturally squared nature of all-bead weaving. Effects can be quite subtle if you use a fiber that is close in value and tint to the bead work. Conversely, strong contrast between beads and fiber can create striking effects that really define the design.

In this bracelet size **6° Czech beads were woven seven-beads wide** on a warp of lightweight but sturdy nylon cord. The bright red start and end of the piece are woven in simple tabby with a doubled ply of size 10 perle cotton.

When the weave was complete, prior to removing the piece from the loom, **one row of soumak weave was stitched between each row of beads** with size 10 perle cotton on a tapestry needle. The thread ends were left long enough to secure within the front of the soumak from both directions. Doing this plumped up the weave and textured it for prominence.

A very slim swipe of glue is dabbed on the threads prior to pulling them through the soumak; the threads are secured using a sharp-pointed darning needle which will slip through the soumak more easily than a blunt-tipped tapestry needle.

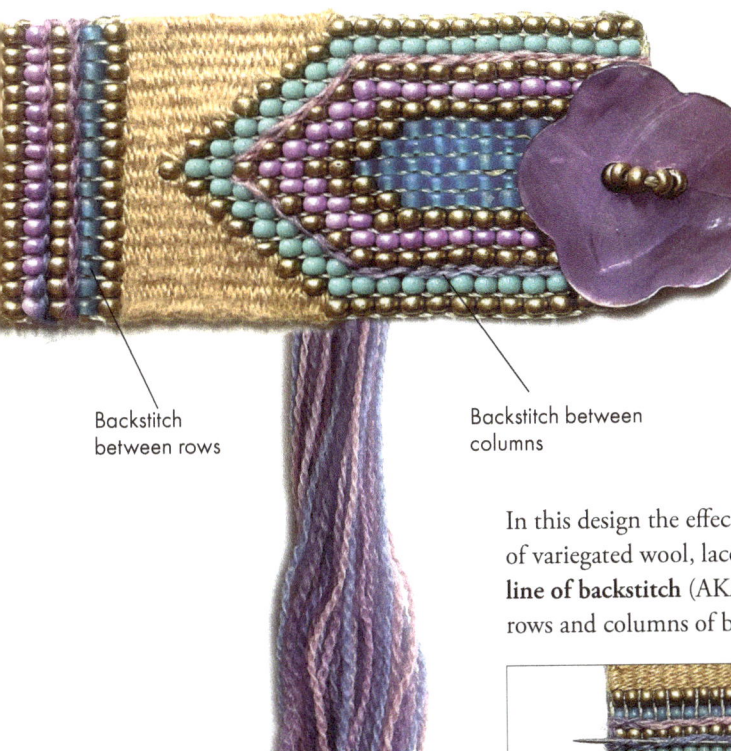

Backstitch
between rows

Backstitch between
columns

In this design the effect is very subtle; the single-ply of variegated wool, lace-weight, is stitched in a **thin line of backstitch** (AKA split stitch) between both rows and columns of beads.

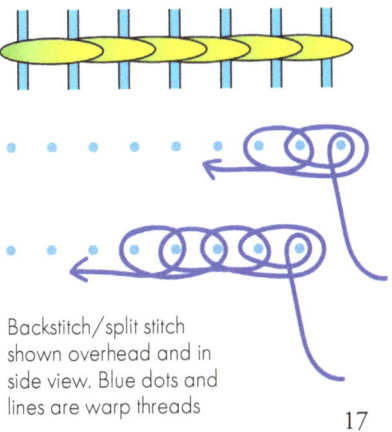

Backstitch/split stitch
shown overhead and in
side view. Blue dots and
lines are warp threads

Mastering the art of the soft pull

Weft-beating device

This is the practice of guiding the weft through the warp in a manner that prevents the warp threads from shifting inward, thereby narrowing the weave. If you're working on a heddle loom, the heddles can keep the warps in place, but on a tapestry or beading loom the edges of the weave are not secured and the weave can shrink inward if you don't pay attention.

This narrowing is almost always the result of pulling the fiber too tightly. This problem is more likely to happen on wide pieces; it's easier to control it in a narrower weave. This takes practice and patience, but there are a few things you can do to mitigate narrowing.

Your choice of warp can make a big difference. A "slippery" warp like nylon upholstery thread will be strong and stable but will minimize friction between the warp and weft. Sturdy cotton warps, while also strong and stable, have microscopic fibers that tug at the weaving thread. Choose a "Goldilocks" warp that won't grip your weft fibers, especially if your project is wide. A bit of trial and error might be involved.

There are devices that can be used to stabilize warps as you pull the fiber through. Some are specifically made for this purpose (beaters, above), and some are everyday items you're likely to have on hand. A small-tooth comb (below, you'll recognize this if you have a pet with fur) is great for fine weaves. Larger everyday hair combs do a marvelous job. **Gently insert the device into the warp before you pull the fiber through and remove it when the pull is complete.**

A fine-tooth comb inserted into a small weave section will stabilize it as you pull the fiber through the warps

Essential needles for tapestry and beading

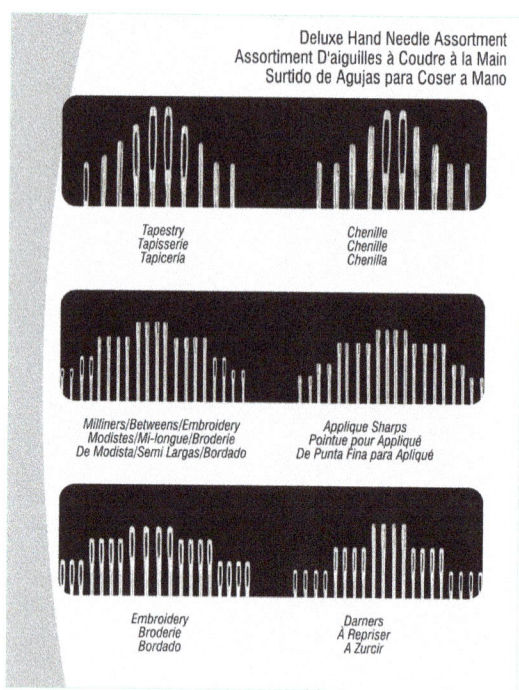
Deluxe Hand Needle Assortment
Assortment D'aiguilles à Coudre à la Main
Surtido de Agujas para Coser a Mano

Tapestry
Tapisserie
Tapicería

Chenille
Chenille
Chenilla

Milliners/Betweens/Embroidery
Modistes/Mi-longue/Broderie
De Modista/Semi Largas/Bordado

Applique Sharps
Pointe pour Appliqué
De Punta Fina para Apliqué

Embroidery
Broderie
Bordado

Darners
À Repriser
A Zurcir

Essential needles for fibers include tapestry needles, darning needles, and large plastic needles.

Tapestry needles with strong shafts have smooth points and do not catch on fibers easily. An advantage of using a tapestry needle in weaving is that you are very unlikely to pierce your warp.

Chenille needles are similar to tapestry needles but have wider eyes and can carry heavier fibers.

Darning needles have sharp points and narrower eyes than tapestry needles; they're great for securing and burying threads on the back of your work. These needles tend to be longer than tapestry needles which in a wide piece can be an advantage.

Large plastic needles are bright, colorful and fun, but these are some of the only needles that will accept a bulky yarn or cut leather for weaving. They're essential for weaving cut strips of fabric.

Almost everything you need in needles for fiber can be found in a deluxe hand-sewing needle assortment.

Beading needles are chosen for the size of the bead. For 15° seed beads, use size 12 or 13 beading needles. Both break easily so have additional on hand. For 11° seed beads and size 11 cylinder beads use size 10 or 12 beading needles. Japanese 11°s can generally be woven with size **10 or 12 embroidery needles.** For sizes 8° and 6°, you can default to size 10 and larger embroidery needles with their slightly larger eyes.

Gloving needles are essential for stitching through leather and non-wovens; I mostly use size 10 and 12, but for heavier leathers such as those you might use in constructing a purse, a larger size 6 or 8 glover can be used.

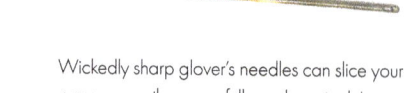
Wickedly sharp glover's needles can slice your warp so use them carefully and sparingly!

Tools that will enhance your tapestry life

Small pliers, both round and flat nosed, will make maneuvering around your project easier, especially if it's a small piece on a loom with limited hand room. If your hands become tired from handling the needle, pliers can extend your working time.

Small scissors with sharp points will make trimming fibers much easier.

Keeping your needles organized and in good condition is easier with the iconic tomato pincushion. Use the strawberry (which is filled with fine sand) to keep the ends of your pointed needles sharp, and the shafts of your blunted needles clean.

Who knew there were so many different kinds of threads.

Knit/crochet fibers
Needlework fibers
Weaving fibers
Variegated fibers

FINGERING

LACE

DK–SPORT

WORSTED

HAIRY

BULKY

SOCK

Knitting/Crochet Fibers

Knitting and crochet yarns come in multiple weights, colors, and fibers, and are often reflective of the fashion standards of the moment. There are standard yarns that are almost always available, including many weights of cotton. Sometimes when one fashion gives way to the next, a previous yarn style may be phased out. Reason enough to become a yarn hoarder!

Knitting/crochet fibers in this book are identified by their weight category, as this is the one quality that remains consistent over time. Categorizations range from fine lace weight to thick, textured bulky weight, and there can be sub-classifications with each category. We are looming and weaving, so we will focus on the basic qualities of stitches and rows per inch, and wraps per inch.

Some manufacturers name the weight category on the label, or alternately give the number of stitches/rows per inch in knitting with standard needle and hooks sizes. You can usually determine the weight using that number as a guideline. Take a picture of this page and bring it along when you go yarn shopping.

If your project is VERY large you will need to note the fiber's dye lot to match in case you need more. A better approach is to buy more than you need; leftover yarn/thread is a blessing.

Industry standard weight categories:

SPI = Stitches per inch in knitting/needle size

Lace	7-8 SPI	000-2 needles
Fingering/Baby	6-7 SPI	1-3 needles
Sock	5-6 SPI	3-5 needles
DK	5.5 SPI	5-7 needles
Sport	5 SPI	7 needles
Worsted	4 SPI	7-9 needles
Bulky	Varies	large needles

Knitting and crochet yarns are generally put up in skeins, balls, cakes, or hanks. I sometimes wind a skein or hank into a ball or cake for easier storage and handling, though variegations are more visible in skeins and hanks.

Test a yarn's category by wrapping it around a one inch on a pencil, pen, or fat knitting needle and counting the wraps. Shown here are actual size wraps of yarns labeled by the manufacturer as the weight category shown, and the resulting number of wraps (WPI). Use this method for roughly determining the yarn's relative weight if it's not marked. With experience you will develop an innate sense of the yarn's suitability for your specific project.

Lace (30 WPI)

Fingering/Baby (24 WPI)

Sock (22 WPI)

DK (17 WPI)

Sport (15 WPI)

Worsted (12 WPI)

Bulky (10 WPI)

SKEIN

CAKE

BALL

Perle Coton/Perle Cotton/Pearl Cotton

By any spelling it's a workhorse for crochet and weaving. Weights are standardized by the size and number of the threads. For example, 3/2 perle cotton is comprised of two twisted threads, both size 3 (a heavy weight). The finer sizes (8/2, 12/2, 16/2) can be combined in multiples to create special effects (perhaps the perfect gradient) and very specific thickness.

5/2

10/2

12/2

16/2

20/2

Variegated fibers

One of the qualities I cherish most in variegated fibers is the sheer unpredictability of outcome. Until you lay the fibers onto the weave, you really don't know what you'll get.

That said, a bit of planning can shade your outcome in the desired direction. How wide is your project? How long are the color bands in the variegation? A bit of simple math can convey an idea of how the color bands will develop.

The examples on this page, all made from the yarns in the photo, were all a delight to weave.

MANY DIFFERENT WEIGHTS OF VARIEGATED FIBER

The very fine lace-weight yarn below has long and subtle variegations. In a narrow weave or a short section of a wider weave the color variations might not develop as you'd expect. I would envision using this type of yarn as a background on which beads would be stitched as embellishments. Its real color story would not emerge unless the weaving section was large and wide enough to span a few color changes.

22

These three variegated yarns have long color bands.

Silk embroidery fibers with short and abrupt variegations

Weaving, needle arts and knit/crochet yarns all come in these wonderful multi-color blended styles. Variegated fibers, while gorgeous, present both design opportunities AND design challenges. Your choice of yarn will be guided by the answers to these two questions: how wide is the variegation relative to the width of my project, and what is my design objective for that woven area?

These three variegated yarns all have shorter color bands.

Multicolor fibers are a feast for the eyes and can add so much to a woven design. In this narrow example two colors of Tencel, one solid, one variegated, the pick and pick section has high contrast to the lighter solid area.

The three weaves shown here use the same variegated lace-weight silk/wool blend on identical warps, all similarly compressed. The color variegation bands are closely spaced in the widest sample section, and most widely spaced on the narrowest.

Variegated ribbon that compresses to create a textured weave with subtle color shifts

You wouldn't guess there are only three fibers in this piece. The variegations give an impression of many colors, especially in the ribbon section.

Needlepoint/Embroidery Fibers

Stitchers and weavers are breaking the mold by using traditional stitchery fibers in exciting contemporary ways—silks, metallics, viscose, rayon, wool, cotton, ribbons, chenille, and even leather. These are just a few examples of the amazing range of fibers available.

SILK/WOOL BLENDS

TAPESTRY WOOL

3-PLY PERSIAN

CREWEL WOOL

6-PLY EMBROIDERY FLOSS

Silken straw is a "flat" multi-strand silk fiber pressed together from less-processed silk fibers. This really lovely fiber can be found in needle work put-ups of very small hanks, or in skeins for knitting. Weavers and knitters will often wind cakes from the skeins. As with 60/2 silk, use shorter strands for this fiber to retain its sheen and texture. I generally use a 36" strand on a large-eye tapestry needle when weaving with this straw.

Silk floss, shown at right in three variegated colors, is similar to cotton floss; some varieties have seven fine strands twisted together instead of the six in cotton floss. As with other silks, strands should not exceed 40" in length to preserve the sheen and luster of the fibers.

Unlike knitting/crochet/weaving yarns, which are often sold in put-ups for larger projects, **needle work and stitchery fibers are most often sold in 8 to 10 yard/meter hanks or skeins.**

Cotton embroidery floss has six plies and can be used intact or separated. You can blend colors with exquisite results (the perfect gradient!). Use all six plies or combine more than six, in one color or multiple colors. Floss is also available in variegated colors, metallics, and rayon.

Wool needlepoint fibers come in three main styles: Persian three-ply wool used for needlepoint and sometimes oriental rugs, **tapestry wool**, which has a weight roughly the same as sport knitting yarn, and fine, soft **crewel embroidery wool**. The color range in these weights often runs into multiple hundreds. Colors used in vintage canvas work and embroidery are typically "European" in that they lean toward the natural dye color palette of the late middle ages and Renaissance. Contemporary dying methods have yielded a much broader palette.

As with knitting and crochet threads, **dye lot issues should inform your purchasing habits.**

Machine embroidery threads can also be used for weaving, usually in multiple plies. These 40/2-weight threads are very widely available in the sewing thread section of most big-box stores and are put up on spools and small tubes. The color range is very good.

Weaving/Tapestry Fibers

I hardly know where to begin. Threads and yarns intended specifically for weaving typically come in larger volume cone, cake or tube put-ups because weaving projects can suck up A LOT of yardage. Color ranges tend to be more limited than needle work threads; there are nearly 500 colors of DMC floss but about 40 colors of Hasegawa silk. That said, weaving fibers are incredibly versatile and are a joy to use.

Weaving yarns are often identified by SETT or EPI (ends per inch) to indicate thickness, similar to the weight categories in knitting yarn.

Perle cotton is generally sold on larger cones for weaving. That said, size 5/2 is often available as an embroidery thread, and crochet cotton comes in ball put-up, usually white or ecru for traditional doilies, tablecloth, and bed covers. You can color this fiber with permanent fabric markers or diluted acrylic paints, always following the manufacturer's recommendations.

Tencel is a natural cellulose (wood) fiber, generally available on cones. It has not yet become popular as a stitchery fiber (not sure why!) so smaller put-ups are not as readily available. Tencel has a slightly "woolly" texture with a soft luster and the colors are generally muted.

Wool and wool blends come in various weights; alpaca and silk blends weave beautifully. Some of the most spectacular variegations can be found in this kind of thread.

60/2 silk thread (Hasegawa shown at right) weaves up in a soft, supple fabric and is often used for scarves, shawls, and neck wear. The fibers are very strong but also **very** fine. In a tapestry-type of weaving project, you'd certainly want to combine multiple strands. The single silk fiber in this weight is roughly similar to ONE ply of six-ply cotton floss or ONE ply of multi-ply silk floss. Work in fairly short strand lengths to preserve the luster of the fiber.

25

Chroma has a variety of fibers and weave methods; to gather these fibers I literally grabbed a number of hanks/balls/skeins of fibers and pulled out a weavable length. I repeated some of the finer fiber areas wide enough to allow decoration.

This was a kind of "bead embroidery" as much as tapestry.

Crafts and techniques using fibers and beads often intersect in beautiful ways.

Making and using a cartoon

A "cartoon" is a simple method for creating guidelines of your design idea on or behind the stretched warp before weaving. This technique is especially useful with upright/standing looms, as the cartoon itself can be positioned behind the warp and left in place without getting in the way of the weaving.

With smaller looms and tabletop looms you may prefer (as do I) to sketch design guides directly onto the warp after your warp is FULLY tensioned. In this example I doodle-wove most of the foreground and then used a cartoon for the sky and sun area.

I held a piece of paper behind the working weave and with my left hand, then dotted the outer points of the area to be cartooned with my right. I removed the paper from behind the weave and connected the dots to form an outline of the desired area. The design was sketched in, and the paper placed behind the open warp area. I used a light-neutral permanent marker to sketch in the guides on the tight warp.

Paper is held behind the warp/weave. Dots (red) are placed to delineate the area to be cartooned

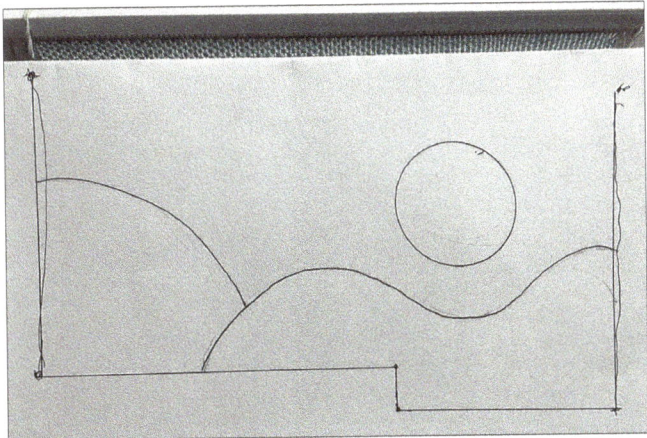

Lines are sketched on the paper within the outlined area.

The weave is added within the sketched guidelines. The weave is added within the sketched guidelines

27

A loom that masquerades as a cartoon, and vice versa.

This design was woven without a traditional or no-finish loom. We covered this a bit in the opening section. In theory the technique of weaving on a bendable plastic sheet is like a no-finish loom in that the warp was secured through slots in the outer edges, and when the weave was removed, there were only two warp ends that needed to be secured.

The two cartoons at right were **printed on uncut adhesive label stock** and applied to Grafix or a similar brand of 20-point plastic.

The shapes were cut from the plastic, leaving a small margin all around. Corners are slightly round to minimize snagging.

The lines at the narrow ends are slit with sharp scissors. The warp is secured to the first slit on either end.

The warp is applied to the slitted plastic in the same manner as for a no-finish loom; the warp is tightened evenly as it's applied so the plastic piece takes on a slight curve. This is a form of tensioning and will yield a neater result. Masking tape is applied to the slit ends to keep the warp in place, though this is not shown in the photos for clarity.

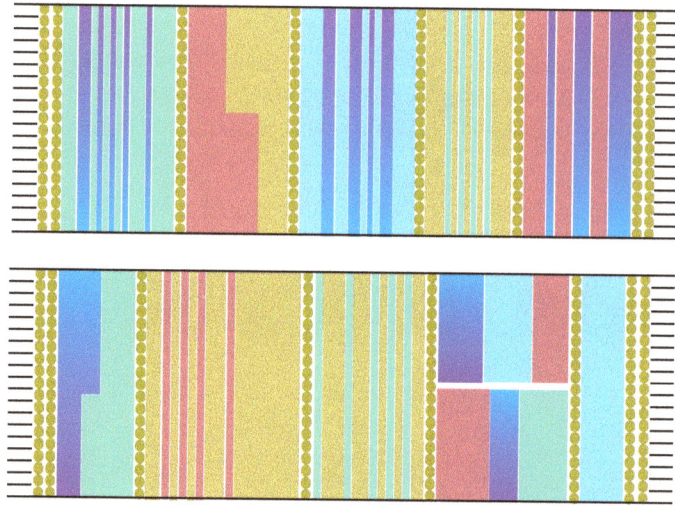

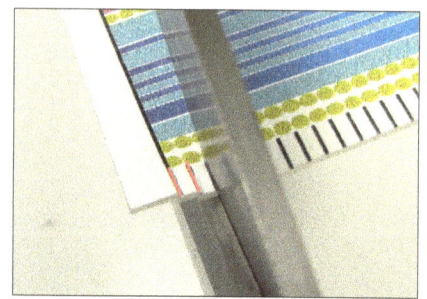

The warp forces a curve on the "loom." Masking tape can minimize thread snagging in the slits.

Thread is attached to the outside warp; the weave is begun away from the end, and as it progresses, the weave is compressed against the slit ends.

Weaving progresses over the printed cartoon, using the shapes and colors as a guide for fiber and bead placement.

After removing the finished piece from the "loom" it may need some form of support. A good choice is non-woven, either medium or heavy weight depending on the end use of your piece.

Here, the two sides are attached to a focal piece, in this case a bezeled cabochon, and a backing is cut in the same shape.

Non-woven is basted to the woven piece; basting stitches are removed later. The non-woven keeps the weave stable and makes it much easier to add a backing.

The end warps make a good attachment point for finishing materials and closures. Here the needle is slipped through one of the end loops and then through the non-woven support and Ultrasuede backing.

Beads on the warp

Beads can be loaded onto the warp thread prior to placing the warp onto the loom. In the multi-color pick-and-pick bracelet as well as the brown-rust-olive bracelet, the two center-most warps were passed through 6° seed beads so the number of warps would be even. The weave was split at the bead locations and continued across the warp where there were no beads. This can take a bit of planning, as you will need to determine how many beads to add prior to warping. You won't be able to add any more once the warp is in place, unless you UN-warp and start all over. I have done this many times, it's not as painful as you might think.

In this case, the beads were grouped in spans of three, and the weave was worked around the spans. The tab end with buttons is simple tabby weave that forms a firm and secure place for the buttons to be sewn.

The warp was begun at the center of the loom (below); this requires estimating the total length of warp you will need and placing its center at the middle of the loom. Warping is continued outward on both sides of the center beaded rows symmetrically until the desired overall width is achieved, after which the warp is secured.

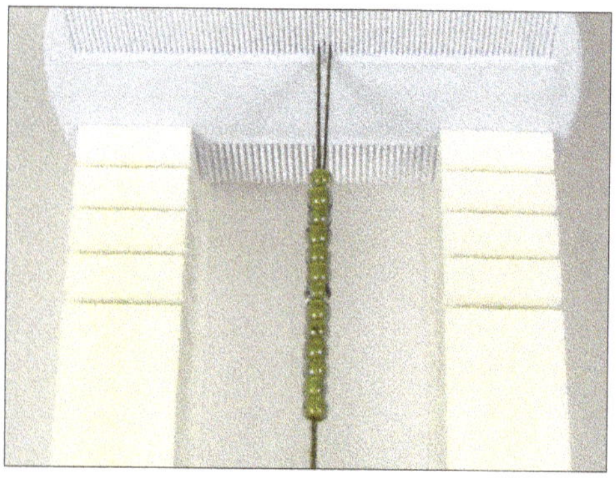

Incorporating bugle beads into the warp prior to weaving can yield really interesting results. The effect can be stepped (left) or straight across depending on how other beads and fibers are woven around the bugles. The project at right has only ten warp threads, with four sets of dark blue bugle beads on the warp at the start. The bugles become "warp" themselves in that seed beads are woven in using the bugles as a base.

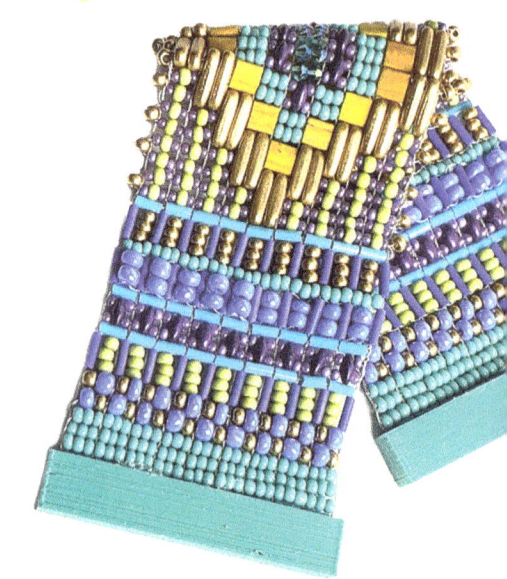

30

Beads can be added to the warp so they fall outside the weaving area if you are using a no-finish loom.

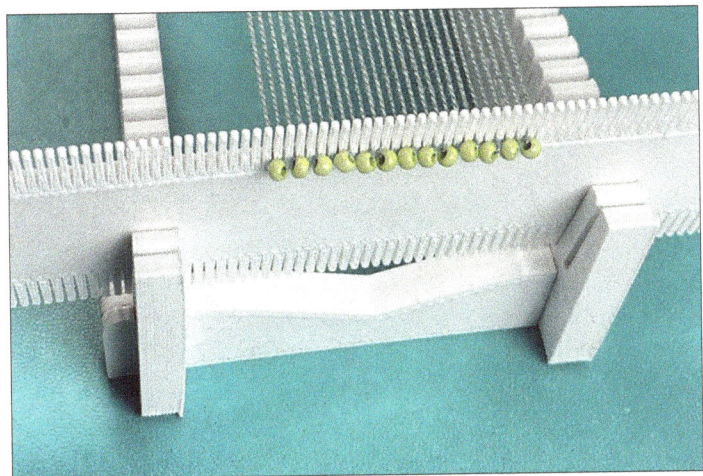 

In this example the 8° beads are loaded onto the warp thread and then positioned on the OUTSIDE of the prongs on a no-finish loom. When the weave is removed and decompressed, the 8° beads serve as an attachment point for the beaded cabochons group and as a neat, attractive finish for the end of the woven strips.

In *Rose Drape* the **gemstone tubes and heishi are threaded onto the warp thread** prior to warping the no-finish loom, with 8° seed beads on the outside end of the loom. The pre-threaded beads are pushed away from the end of the weave and incorporated later between tows of 11° seed beads.

This presentation of beads on the warp is quite simple in this example but you can certainly add more complex threadings. In general, **pre-threading beads onto the warp thread makes the warping process take longer** than a simple unbeaded warp, but the **weaving time is minimized**.

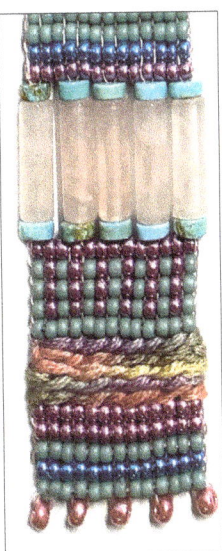 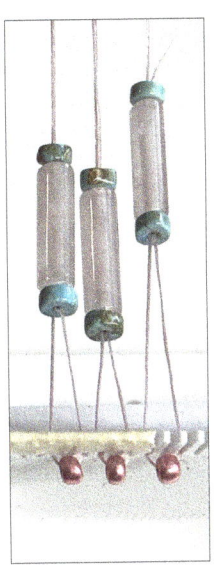

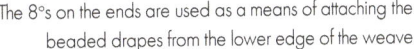

The 8°s on the ends are used as a means of attaching the beaded drapes from the lower edge of the weave

A silken sampler

15º opaque pale green

15º opaque light banana

15º opaque lustered pumpkin

15º opaque light ocher

15º opaque light sea green

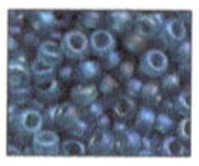

15º opaque matte turquoise AB

In this one woven strip there are several different basic and simple weave techniques using a variety of silk fibers. There are thirty-six (36) warps in this piece yielding thirty-five (35) bead spaces.

The fiber weaves are combined randomly with patterned spans of 15º seed beads in repeating patterns. All of the seed beads in this sampler are Japanese in a combination of Miyuki and Toho.

Charts for all of the beaded patterns used in this piece are included at the end of this book.

Silk straw

Silk 30% Alpaca 70%

Silk straw

Caron 12-ply silk

6-ply silk floss

Silk straw

2/60 silk Hasegawa

2/60 silk Hasegawa

The descriptions to the right of the enlarged photo give details about how to add each section.

All of the fibers used in this design are silk or partly silk; this wonderful natural fiber is by far my favorite. It's not the easiest fiber to weave, especially in the very fine weights such as 60/2, which really must be used multi-strand.

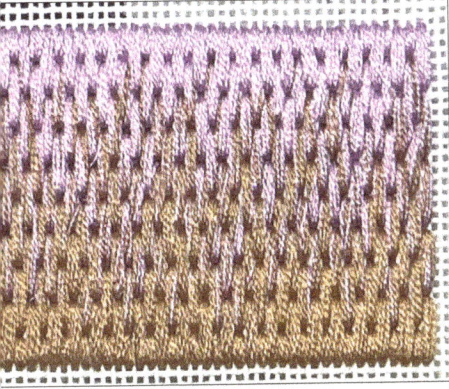

This section of 60/2 silk used multi-strand on size 18 needlepoint canvas shows how a beautiful gradient can be created by combining strands of very fine silk.

Six plies are used in each weaving thread, starting with all six the same color, then five of that color and one of the next shade, then four of that color and two of the next shade, and so on until all six plies are the other color. The same technique can be used to create perfect gradients in weaving by combining strands

Start with two rows of tabby over one in silken straw doubled (this secures the warp) then switch to plain tabby over two for texture.

Lace -weight wool variegated single ply, plain tabby over two warps

Perle cotton size 10, single ply, plain tabby over one warp

Soumak weave in fingering-weight silk, filled in after weaving the 15°s

Soumak in opposite directions sandwiching single row of 15°s, variegated wool single ply

Perle cotton size 10, single ply over one warp
Pick & pick on two warps, alternating colors
Perle cotton size 10, single ply over one warp

Three rows soumak in four plies of 60/2 silk thread

Three rows of soumak, one sock-weight variegated cotton, one five cylinder beads in each span, another using sock-weight cotton.

Ten rows of pick and pick, alternating aqua and orange silken straw, doubled, over one warp. Very loosely compressed to create this look.

Lace -weight wool variegated single ply, plain tabby over two warps

Backstitch weave over one warp using four plies of 60/2 silk thread

Silken straw doubled, over two warps in plain tabby, moderately compressed

Sock-weight long-variegation cotton in simple tabby weave over one warp, heavily compressed

Six-ply cotton floss, softly variegated, simple tabby weave over one warp

33

Designs & Projects

I sincerely hope you will enjoy the designs in this book. Some are vintage and brought back to life. Many are new and created entirely for this book.

I've loved working with a really unique and inspiring range of materials and styles and I hope you will, as well.

Nepali

BEADS with symbols

 Miyuki 11° 1233 opaque matte mustard (620)

 Delica 653 opaque burnt orange (56)

 Toho 12° three-cut 332 lustered claret (721)

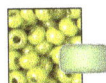 Czech 11° BL1076 lustered pale olive (98)

 Toho 15° 246 crystal lined pale olive (366)

 Czech 14° 17050 sil-ver-lined topaz (230)

 Czech11° 53490 opaque olive (340)

 Toho 11° 940 transparent deep olive (147)

 Czech 8° 59439 met-al-lined citrine AB (35)

High-dome round cabochon 20mm
Olive pearls 6-7mm (2)
Mustard pearls 5-6mm (2)
Claret pearls 6mm (2)
6mm round crystal garnet (2)
4mm bicone crystal garnet (2)
4mm bicone crystal lime AB (17)

FIBERS USED

 Lace-weight wool (6 two-yd/m lengths)

 Silken straw (4 two yd/m lengths)

 Sport-weight gold (2 lengths)

 Size 10 perle cotton (6 lengths)

 Alpaca silk lace-weight (2 lengths)

 Size 10 perle cotton (8 lengths)

A no-finish loom is recommended; size D beading nylon can be used for both warping and bead weaving.

This design is woven in two strips, joined at the center front by one warp loop. The length of the warp is 8.25" (21 cm). Additional sizing is done by adjusting button placement. The sett is 14-15 warps per inch to accommodate 11° beads.

Cut a length of warp 8 yd/m long. Put a needle on one end and load seven (7) 8°s, one garnet round, and seven (7) more 8°s onto the warp thread. Secure one end of the warp, leaving a tail of about 5". Wrap the warp around the prongs/rod at the opposite end, slipping one 8° bead to the outside of the prong/rod before pulling the warp through. Do not add 8° beads at the other (buttonhole) end. Continue in this manner until you have twelve (12) warp threads.

Slip one 8°, the round, and another 8° (replacing one 8°) which will land at the center of the weave. Continue warping, adding 8°s to each bottom prong/rod on one end and no beads on the other end. Secure the warp end and trim, leaving a tail of 5-6". You now have twenty-eight (28) warps with beads on one end.

The full woven strips are mirrored and joined at the center of the base with a bridge of one 8º, one round, and another 8º. The 8º beads at the base serve as anchors for the weaves to be joined to the "wings" that surround the bezeled cabochon.

Fringes are added at the base of the wings and cabochon.

Three buttonholes allow for adjustments in sizing. If more length is needed, you can omit the buttonholes and use an adjustable mechanical clasp of your choosing.

This design was worked from the bottom edge upward on the loom.

Step 1 Surround the cabochon in a bezel of 11°s, Delicas and 15°s. Use peyote stitch in the round (appendix). On a forty inch (40") nylon thread, pick up fifty-six (56) ocher 11°s and form a ring by running back through several beads; center the ring on the thread. The ring of beads will just fit around the round stone (1A).

Add one round of 11°s. Since the initial ring forms the first TWO rounds, you will now have three rounds of 11°s (1B).

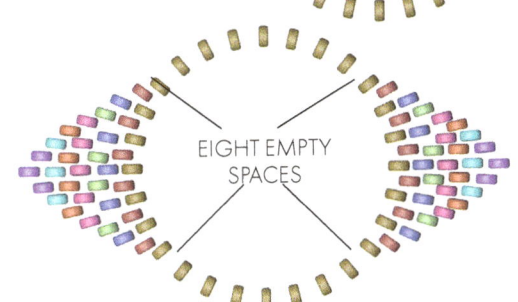

Add one round of Delicas (1C); the ring is now slightly shaped. Add a second round of Delicas (1D). **Complete the front of the bezel** with one round of 15° 246 and one round of 14° 17050 (1E). Secure the top thread and trim it.

Prepare the bezel for the addition of the wing bases. First, add two groups of six 11°s, with eight empty space between the groups. The 11°s are added in the third row down of 11°s, shown dotted RED in the photo.

Flip the bezel over and bring the thread out of any 11° in the outermost round. **Add one round of 11° 1233.** Place the cabochon face down in the bezel and **add one round of Delicas** (1F), drawing in the bezel as you progress. Add one round of 15° 246, again drawing in the bezel. Complete the back with one round of 14°s (1G), then add the wing bases (below).

THIRD ROW DOWN DOTTED RED

EIGHT EMPTY SPACES

EIGHT EMPTY SPACES

Step 2 Create the "wings" symmetrically on the sides of the bezel. Build the wings on the groups of six 11°s just added. An overview is shown in 1G; steps are shown in (1H, 1I). Black thin lines indicate established thread path; heavier red lines indicate the thread path added in that step.

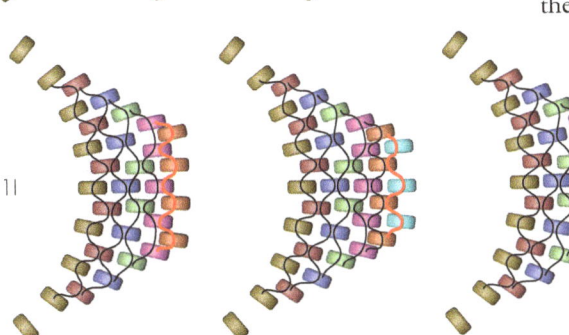

1H

1I

Use a thin needle in stitching the wings, preferably a size 13 beading needle. To reverse direction, catch the thread of the previous pass (1J), rather than weaving into the bezel.

1J

The complete beaded wings. You can straighten the outer edges if needed by running a continuous thread from one side to the other. Secure the thread and trim it.

STEP 3 Weave the neck straps. This design is symmetrical/mirrored; only one neck strap will be shown; the other strap is woven in mirror image. You will work on only fourteen warps for each side.

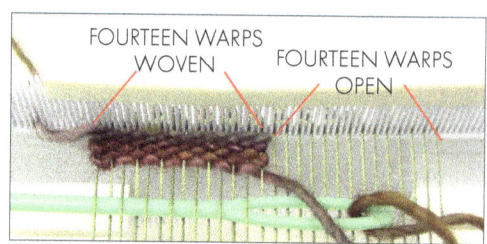
FOURTEEN WARPS WOVEN
FOURTEEN WARPS OPEN

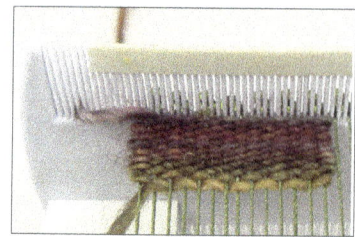

Begin at the end with the 8's; use a full strand of variegated wool. Start on the outside and weave in basic tabby for twenty rows (about 3/8"), compressing the weave as you progress with the needle as each row is added. Your thread will be on the outside. Do not cut or secure the thread.

Weave one row of gold fiber in plain tabby directly after the twentieth row of variegated. Leave a 4" tail on the outside edge. Now you will switch to pick and pick weave with the variegated wool 20 rows so the entire weave is about 3/4" in compressed length.

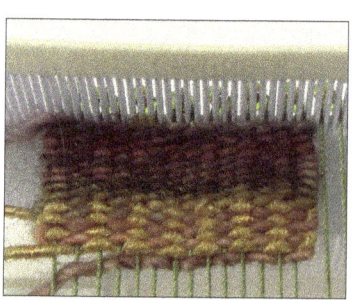

With the variegated thread tail on the outside, **continue in gold only for fourteen (14) rows.** Catch the variegated thread in the gold as you reverse direction in each row, so the variegated thread will be secured when you trim it.

Trim the variegated thread close to the weave, taking care not to cut weaving or warp threads. Glue can be used SPARINGLY on the cut end to keep it in place. Cut the gold thread, leaving a five inch (5") tail which you will secure later.

Add the first bead section. Attach a one-yard nylon beading thread to the outside warp, leaving a five inch (5") tail. You'll find it easier to start a bit out from the gold fiber weave; be sure not to pierce the warp with the weaving needle because you will need to compress the bead weaving against the gold fiber weave. Check as you progress to make sure the beads move. Continue weaving until the entire bead section is complete, as always trying to avoid piercing the warp threads with the needle.

You'll notice that the beaded section is narrower than the fiber section. Larger beads will be added to the edging at the beaded sections to create a neat-looking edge.

When the beaded section is complete, secure the ending tail within the beaded section and trim it. Leave the starting tail intact until finishing, later.

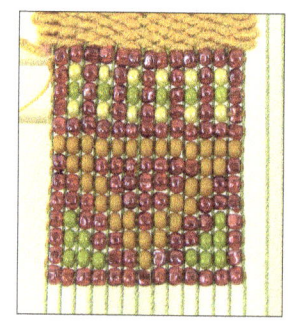

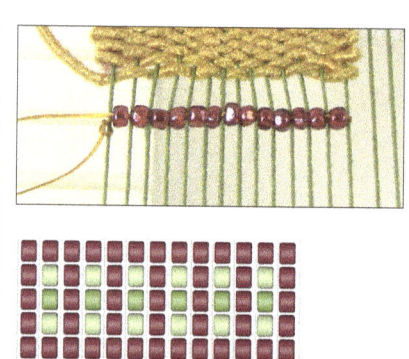

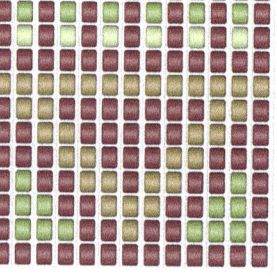

Switch to silken straw fiber. Loop a full strand on the outside warp. Even the ends so the entire length is doubled. Put a needle on the doubled strand.

Start by passing the thread OVER the outermost warp and under the second, and weave six full rows of over under. Compress this section loosely, you'll compress it more fully shortly.

Weave six rows on the six outside warps.

Weave six rows on the ten outside warps.

Weave twelve rows on the four outside warps, leaving six to eight inches of doubled thread left. Separate the two ends and secure each one into the work separately, then bring the end to the back and trim, taking care not to cut fibers.

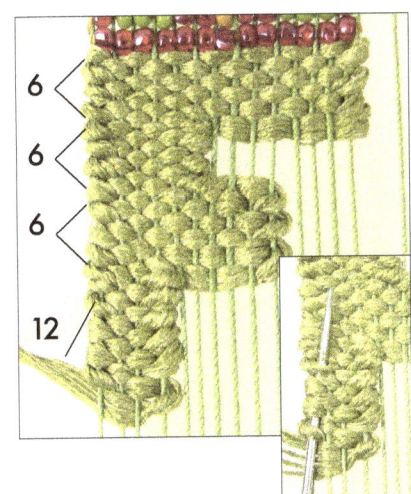

Loop a full strand of alpaca silk on the inside warp of the fourteen warp side. Even the ends. Weave the doubled strand EIGHT rows on the eight interior warps (alpaca compresses more than straw; more rows are needed in the same space). Compress the weave; weave EIGHT rows on four warps, then FOURTEEN rows on ten warps. Rotate the loom as needed to make weaving easier. Secure the two ends separately as with the straw. This section will not be attractive now but will improve as you continue.

Weave the fourteen-row section of beads. Secure and trim the starting and finishing ends of the nylon.

Start a full length of variegated wool at the outside of the fourteen-warp section and weave in tabby over TWO warps across the full fourteen warps until you have twelve rows. Secure and trim the wool.

Weave the five-row beaded section, followed by sixteen (16) rows of tabby over TWO in variegated wool. Add the seven-row beaded section following the variegated wool.

Begin the pick and pick section with ten rows of tabby over TWO in ocher cotton. Add a single strand of variegated and alternate the cotton and wool in pick and pick for eighteen total rows or until there is about 5" of ocher left for securing. Continue for eight rows of tabby over TWO in variegated wool alone. Secure and trim threads.

Weave the final beaded section with nylon beading thread, then secure and trim the threads. Weave twelve rows of over-under over one warp with variegated, then secure and trim the threads.

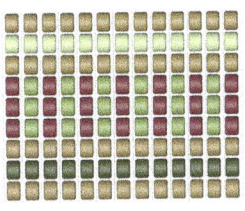

STEP 4 Weave the buttonhole end. Start at the outer end of the warp. If your neck is larger than 16", you can add a loop at the end of the weave to catch the button rather than overlapping the ends. Loop a doubled strand of dark olive cotton on the outer-most warp. Weave ten full rows of plain tabby, then nineteen rows on only seven warps, ending with the thread on the inside. You can secure the thread end later.

Loop an ocher cotton thread inside the open seven warps.

Weave eighteen rows of doubled ocher cotton over seven warps. In the nineteenth row, weave across the entire fourteen-warp span; continue for five total rows. In row 6, weave over seven warps to start the next buttonhole. Continue for a total of nineteen short rows, ending with the thread in the center.

Loop a dark olive cotton thread in the center and **weave a section of dark olive** in the same manner as for the ocher, ending with the thread in the center.

Complete the buttonhole section with a last thread of ocher cotton, weaving eighteen short rows and five or more full rows. You may need more or less depending on how the previous weave has landed on the warp and you may need to add another thread to finish; this will vary according to tension and compression.

Three buttonholes make this necklace highly adjustable for fit. Before sewing the button in place, try on the necklace and determine the best placement for your specific size. When you've sewn the button in place, you can stitch the open buttonholes on the button side closed if desired.

STEP 5 Weave the opposite side in mirror image (shown below smaller than actual size). Take care not to catch the completed side in your needle as you weave the new side; this is especially likely to happen when weaving with a sharp-pointed needle. The photo that follows shows the full woven area 90% of actual size. The two sides are not perfectly matched; this is because the designer is pathetically right-handed. Yours will not be perfect either. You're in good company.

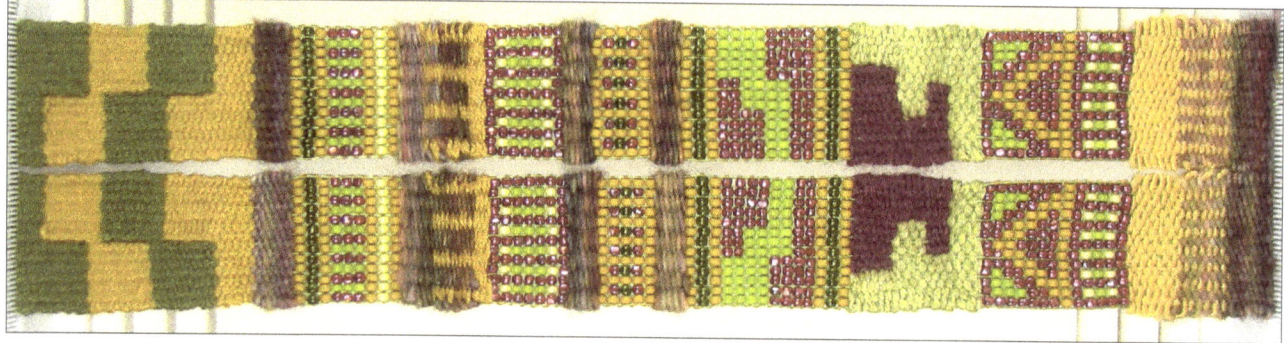

STEP 6 Remove the buttonhole end from the loom. The two sides will separate. Decompress to cover any visible warps. Choose your preferred side as the front and secure thread ends on the other side of the weave, then trim excess threads.

Remove the beaded end carefully. Put a needle on the warp end(s) and run the warp end through the warp loops carrying beads and through the 8°, round, and 8° group in the center. Run through the warp loops of the other side, then trim. Repeat this with the other loose warp thread. Take out the slack but don't pull so hard that the end is distorted. Decompress the weave so the loops disappear.

STEP 7 Attach the bezeled cabochon to the center front.
The 8°-round-8° group is at the center top of the bezel and
the six other 8°s are used to attach the bezel and wings. All
attachments are made in the second-from back round of
11°s in the bezel, same as the wings. Loops of 14° 17050
run through the 8°s of the group and the six 8°s on the warp
loops of the woven end.

Five of the inner loops
have three 14°s on each
side; the outer two loops
have four or five 14°s
as illustrated. Adjust as
needed to create a flat lay
in the assembly.

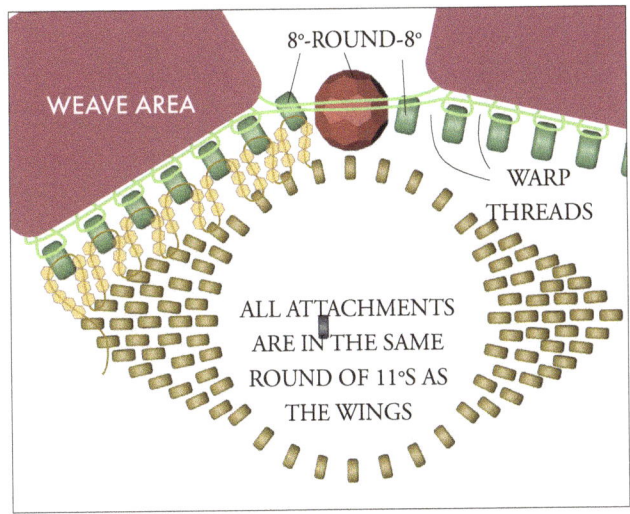

STEP 8 Add the decorations and fringes. Add the gold pearl, garnet bicone, claret pearl, and
seed bead decorations along the outer edges of both sides. The thread path is shown at left; note
how the depth of the thread path varies in the beaded areas. When adding decorations within the
woven areas, keep the nylon beading thread invisible within the fibers.

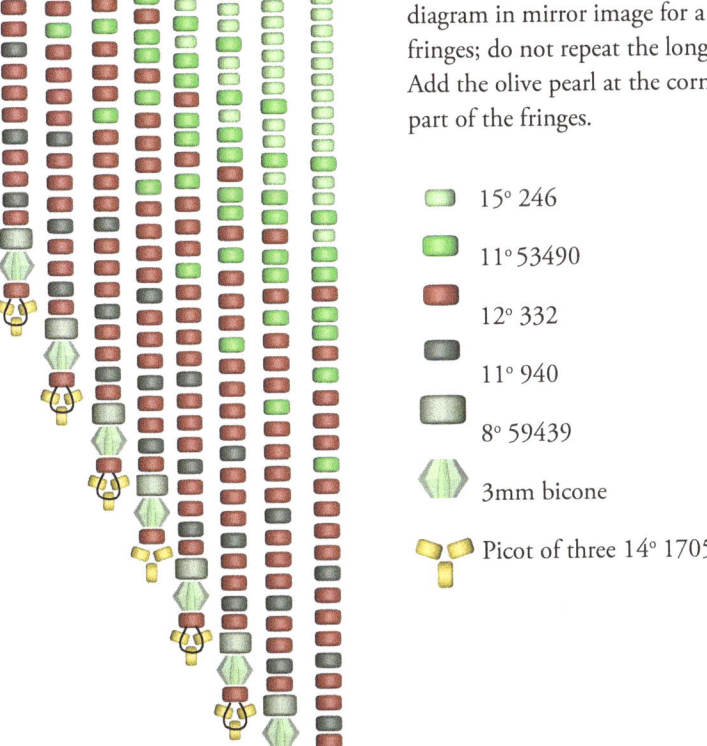

Add one round of 15°
246 in the second round
from top of 11° 1233 on
the bezel.

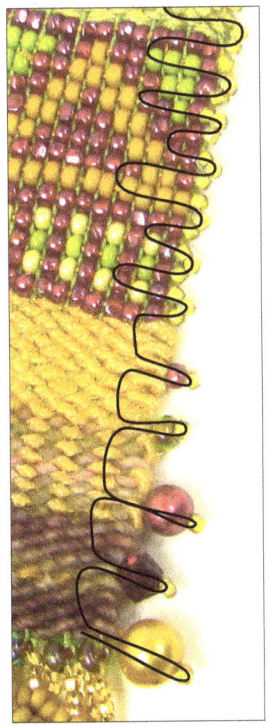

Following the diagram, **add fifteen fringes** in the
second-from-bottom round of 11° 1233 on the
bezel and the lower edge of the wings. Repeat the
diagram in mirror image for a full set of chevron
fringes; do not repeat the longest center fringe.
Add the olive pearl at the corner of the wing as
part of the fringes.

- 15° 246
- 11° 53490
- 12° 332
- 11° 940
- 8° 59439
- 3mm bicone
- Picot of three 14° 17050

STEP 9 Add the closure. Position a
round bead as needed to create the desired
length; you can place a sewing pin as a
marker. If you need more length, use a
mechanical clasp of your choosing. Stitch
the buttonholes closed if desired.

Green and Gold

The stunning strip of **batik fabric** that serves as the background of this bracelet design was hiding in my sewing box for a long time, and I'm glad I hoarded it.

The fibers used are all leftovers, since only a couple of strands of each are needed. The green and blue beads are in finger-pinch amounts, where as the gold, which is used for the edging as well, requires a good amount.

In this weave the **rows of beads are curved and straight**; I filled the gaps between the beads, which were added first, with plain tabby weave over one in four different fibers, two blues and two greens.

Weaving beads

 Japanese 15° seed bead light green (12 beads)

 Japanese 15° seed bead medium green (12 beads)

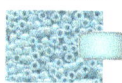 Japanese 15° seed bead light aqua (22 beads)

 Japanese 15° seed bead medium aqua (22 beads)

 Japanese 15° seed bead Duracoat gold (25-30 grams)

Decorative beads

4mm lochrosen or sequins (6)

3mm crystal bicones (24)

Size 2 Czech bugles (24)

4mm round firepolish beads (14)

Use a size 12 beading needle and nylon beading thread for weaving the beads; use a size 12 gloving needle and a doubled nylon thread for the wrapped edging.

 Lace weight wool medium green

 Silk floss 6-ply variegated light aqua

 Lace-weight wool variegated navy-teal

 Lace-weight wool variegated medium aqua

  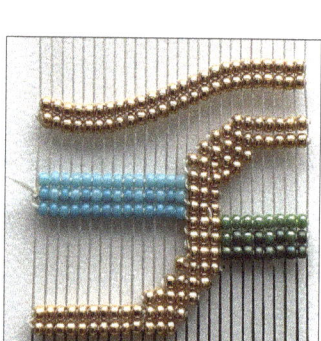

The warp is nylon micro cord. This piece was woven on a traditional loom, and has warp fibers that require finishing. The size of the weave area is 2" (5.8 cm) x 1 3/16" (3 cm) wide.

The sett for the warp is at 22 per inch to accommodate 15° seed beads. The total number of warps on the width is 26 yielding 15 bead spaces.

After warping the loom, weave the beaded motifs. The top gold motif is curved after weaving; just weave two full rows of 25 beads each, keeping your tension fairly loose so you can curve the rows after weaving. In this design I used a permanent marker to color the warp threads before weaving so absolutely no warp threads would show through in the dark areas.

Using plain tabby, weave the fiber areas. Force the two single rows of gold into a curve with the fibers. Weave the upper and lower sections of fiber so the overall length of the woven strip is 2 1/4". This will allow for 1/4" to be wrapped over the top edge of the fabric strip and under the bottom edge prior to finishing.

Cut a strip of heavy-weight non-woven (Pellon 70) 1 3/4"(4.5 cm) wide and as long as you need allowing for your chosen clasp. Using a thin even layer of flexible fabric glue, attach the fabric strip to the non-woven and allow it to dry for at least an hour.

Trim off the excess fabric along the edge of the non-woven and run a thin diluted bead of glue (use a small paintbrush and wash it immediately). This will minimize raveling.

Cut the woven piece off the loom, retaining length on the warp threads.

Wrap the weave around the center of the fabric/non-woven strip and lightly baste the upper and lower edges in place. Secure the cut warp threads within the non-woven, understanding that it will be a hot mess about which you are forbidden to fret. Glue is your ally.

Cut an Ultrasuede or leather strip the same size as the trimmed fabric/non-woven and lightly glue it in place. **Wrap the assembly around a cylindrical object** to dry, noting that the outer ends of the Ultrasuede or leather will be forced outward by the curve. When dry, and after removing the assembly from the cylinder, trim the excess so the outer edges are even.

Decoration can be added before or after the edging; ideally, they are added before you put the backing Ultrasuede in place. If before, allow space on the top and bottom edges of the fabric/non-woven strip for the wrap-around edging. If after, try to keep your back threads as invisible as possible.

A size 12 embroidery needle will work well; anchor each lochrosen with one gold 15°.

Use a doubled thread or make two passes to secure the **bugle/crystal/15°** spans along the sides of the woven panel.

Secure each 4mm round with one 15° gold so they sit in a neat row along the top and bottom edges of the weave.

Using 15° gold, **work a wrap-around edging all around,** (diagrams, right) except the top and bottom edges of the woven strip. Use six or seven beads per wrap. Adjust the wraps at the corners to try to keep them square. Attach your chosen clasp using 15° gold seed beads or glue, as indicated by the type of clasp you chose.

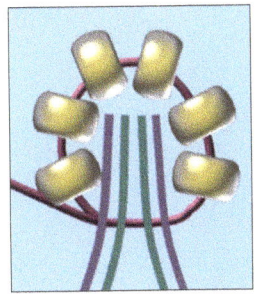
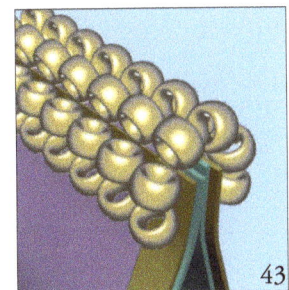

Cocoa Mint

A bezeled jasper cabochon sized 25 x 18mm is stitched to the center panel of this 1.5" wide bracelet. All of the sizing is done in the center area, which is comprised of rows of 8° seed beads with "ribbing" of perle cotton in between.

WEAVING DETAILS NEXT PAGE

The loom is warped with the weaving area set to the same length as your wrist size; this bracelet should fit closely as the center stone will slip to the underside of your wrist. Additional rows are added in creating the toggle clasp, and will overlap at the ends.

Start with **four rows of Delicas on both ends** of the weave; buttonhole and toggle tabs are added later in square stitch (appendix).

After removing the piece from the loom, **add a toggle tab with three decreasing rows of square stitch.** To add the buttonhole start with eight beads on each side, leaving a center gap of eleven beads. Add one full row to create the buttonhole, then decrease by one bead at both sides of each row for three more rows.

Bracelet, 1.5" (3.8mm) wide, variable length

Warp the loom with Size D beading nylon or 30-weight mercerized cotton. Place 28 warps evenly over 1.5" (17-18 sett)

Fibers

 Fingering 4 yd/m
Malabrigo Finito

 Fingering 4 yd/m

 10/2 perle cotton 10 yd/m cocoa

 10/2 perle cotton 14 yd/m soft mint

Beads

 Delica 1151 (2 grams)

 Toho 15° 558PF (112)

 Czech 15° Charlotte sterling (28)

 Matsuno 8° (143)

 Miyuki 11° 2028 (24)

Create a toggle bar in peyote stitch (appendix) 13 rows long by 10 rows (five edge beads) wide. Roll the peyote and zip edges together to create the bar. Decorate the ends of the bar with one 8° at each end anchored with one Toho 15°. Secure the bar to the square stitch area using two Delicas placed centrally on the bar; make a second pass of thread for strength.

SQUARE STITCH PATTERN
FOR BUTTONHOLE

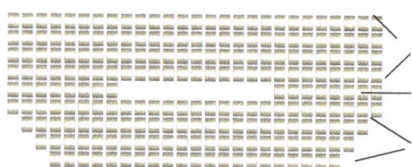

FOUR ROWS AT ENDS

EIGHT BEADS ON SIDES

DECREASING ROWS

The design is symmetrical; slightly more than half is shown, enlarged for clarity.

SINGLE ROWS OF DELICAS BETWEEN FIBER AREAS

After warping the loom, attach a 36" length of nylon thread, which will be carried down the side of the weave so you don't need to add on nylon for the single rows. Weave four rows of Delicas on both ends of the loom; these four rows will form the basis for the closure.

Two rows of soumak weave, in opposite directions

Twenty-four rows, (12 in each direction) of simple over-under weave in soft mint perle cotton

Two rows of soumak weave, in opposite directions

Twenty-four rows, (12 in each direction) of simple over-under weave in coca perle cotton

Two rows of soumak weave, in opposite directions

Twenty-four rows, (12 in each direction) of simple over-under weave in soft mint perle cotton

Two rows of soumak weave, in opposite directions

Sixteen rows of pick and pick over two warps using doubled strands of both colors of perle cotton. The 28 warps will pair up to form fourteen doubled warp threads. The 8° seed beads will fit in these spaces.

Fiber ribbing between rows of 8°s (as on page 17)

When the pick and pick section is complete, **mirror what you have already done.** The open area at the center will vary in length depending on the size of your wrist. Using basic bead weaving, add the number of rows of 8°s needed to fully fill the space. Compress the woven mirrored sections and try to fit in one more row of 8°s. **Weave perle cotton double ribbing between the bead rows for stability and decoration.** Secure all threads and trim them.

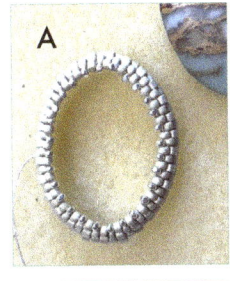

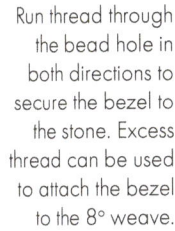

Run thread through the bead hole in both directions to secure the bezel to the stone. Excess thread can be used to attach the bezel to the 8° weave.

Bezel the 25x18mm puff oval bead as follows: Initial ring 56 Delicas, add two more rounds of Delicas for a total of four Delica rounds. Add two rounds of 15° and one round of Czech Charlottes (A). Invert the bezel and insert the bead (B); add two rounds of 15°, ending with one round of Czech Charlottes (C). Position the bezel to your liking, then run a thread through the bead hole in both directions (D) to secure the bezel on the bead prior to mounting on the weave.

Amazonite

Only three fibers are used. Adjustments in sizing are made entirely within the fiber areas.

Actual size 8" woven strip for a large wrist removed from the loom, leather backing glued in place. Closure adds length.

Warp

Slippery nylon micro-cord recommended, twenty (20) warp threads yielding nineteen (19) bead spaces across 1.25" (3.25cm).
The cabochon is 40 x 30mm in a soft square shape; oval can also be used.

Weaving beads

 11° seed beads metallic gold (296)

 11° seed beads matte teal AB (82)

Bezeling beads

 Size 11 cylinders metallic gold (296)

 15° seed beads metallic gold (82)

Finishing materials

Calfskin leather for purse

Non-woven stabilizer

Ultrasuede lining/backing

Button 5/8" (11mm) for bracelet

8° seed beads for purse edging

4mm heishi for strip edging and decoration

 11° seed beads to edge bracelet, metallic gold (300+)

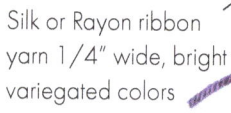

Silk or Rayon ribbon yarn 1/4" wide, bright variegated colors

Fingering/sock weight yarn, dark variegated color

Fingering/sock weight yarn, light variegated color

The weave is created in two separate strips using basic tabby weave and the pick and pick technique. Both strips start and end with beaded sections. Strips are mounted on non-woven for support; if you used a traditional loom the cut warps can be used for mounting.

The separate strips are attached to the non-woven AFTER the stone is bezeled at the center of the non-woven so the innermost edges touch the bezel. The strip is curved to reveal open areas, which are filled with beads. Leather is glued to the threaded side; when dry the excess non-woven and leather are trimmed away. Beaded edging is added and serves as an attachment point for the closure of your choice.

Use this design as a bracelet, a partial hat band, or the closure on a clutch purse.

In both strips, weave the three beaded sections first, taking care not to pierce the warp threads. Position the beaded sections based on your desired sizing. Allow 2" (5mm) for the focal cabochon.

11° seed beads metallic gold (296)

11° seed beads matte teal AB (82)

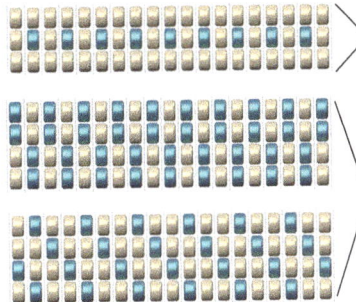

This three-row pattern is used at the start and end of both woven strips

Use either of these four-row patterns in the center of each woven strip

Weave two-thirds of this section in tabby weave with the two halves in different colors. Weave the two colors into each other in alternating rows to avoid a large gap. NOTE: For a button closure, leave a gap large enough for the button, then weave the colors into each other. In the remaining third, use ribbon in tabby weave, compressing it densely to create texture.

ATTACH TO CABOCHON

Weave six rows in one color using tabby weave, then use a second color in pick and pick for ten rows (five each of the two colors). Weave the remaining open area in ribbon, compressing the weave densely to create texture.

Use ribbon in basic tabby weave between the two beaded strips. Compress the weave dramatically to create texture.

Weave this two-color area in tabby, with a multi-row section at the center where the colors intersect to form a step appearance

BUTTONHOLE (if used)

ATTACH TO CABOCHON

JOINING THE STONE AND THE WEAVES

1 Position one woven strip at one end of the non-woven strip. If you are using a buttonhole closure, position it at the outer end. Baste the weave's outer edges to the non-woven with invisible stitches. Stretch and straighten the weave as you progress.

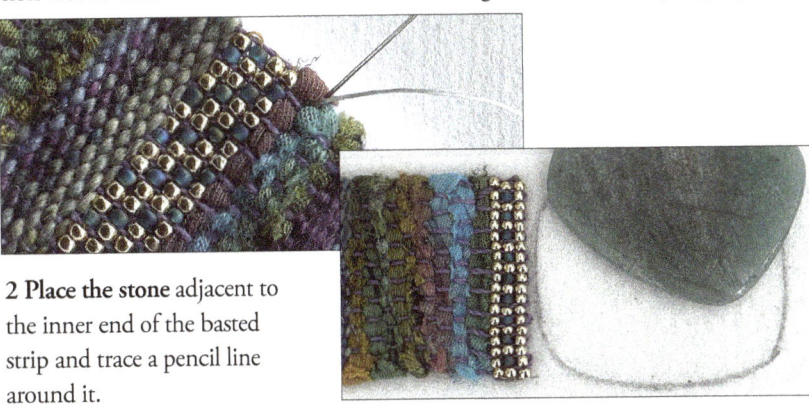

2 Place the stone adjacent to the inner end of the basted strip and trace a pencil line around it.

47

3 Stitch the initial ring of the bezel using cylinder beads in backstitch (appendix), TWO BEADS AT A TIME for an even number of beads. Spread glue evenly inside the ring and insert the stone.

4 Add four full rounds of peyote stitch (**appendix**). In the fifth round, replace three cylinders in each corner with gold 15°s (red dots) to draw in the shape. Complete the bezel with two full rounds of 15°s.

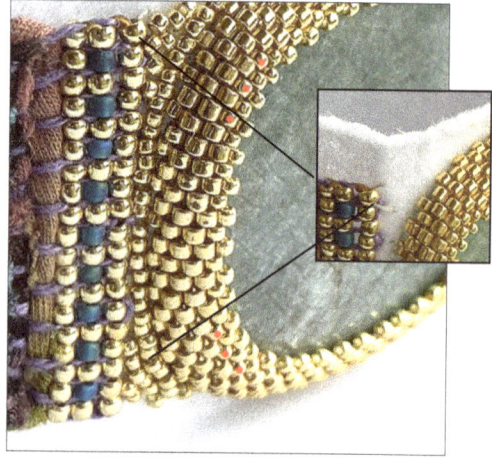

5 Fill the corner gaps. The design is curved so areas between the stone and weave will be exposed when worn. Using 15° gold in backstitch, stitch lines of beads and then fill with individual beads as needed.

6 Secure the other woven strip to the non-woven in the same manner as for the first strip, positioning it so the bracelet will be symmetrical.

7 Glue the leather to the back of the non-woven. Smooth out air bubbles with your fingertips.

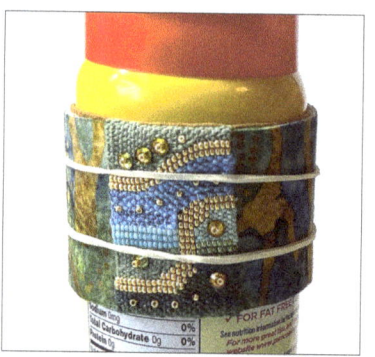

8 (Bracelet) Wrap the glued assembly around a cylindrical object (different design shown) and secure it with elastic bands. Allow to dry for at least two hours, then remove.

9 Trim the leather and excess non-woven close to the edges, taking care not to cut any weaving threads or beading threads. Color the edge carefully with a close color marker.

10 Add a simple beaded edging (appendix) on the long edges only (short ends will be incorporated into the body edging or clasp) using 4mm heishi; when done, decorate each individual heishi with one gold 15°. For a bracelet, use 11° gold for edging on the short ends.

Creating the clutch purse

The woven beaded strip spans the front of this small gusseted purse to create the closure without a mechanical clasp. A magnetic clasp can be added but is not recommended.

The curved lower edge of the flap slips between the purse and the strip. Where it lands will differ depending on the contents of the purse.

Beaded edging stabilizes the outer silhouette of the rounded flap. A span of 4mm heishi is placed directly below the focal area of the strip, mirroring its edging. Prior to adding the purse edging, the nylon beading thread is colored with permanent marker to approximate the leather color.

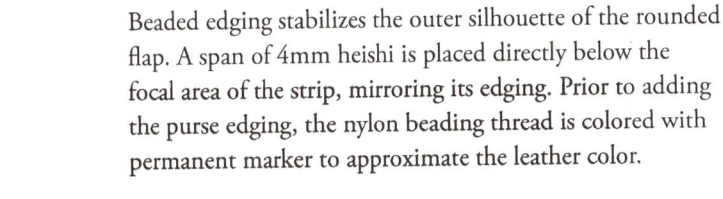

Three card pockets are sewn inside the lining to land on the center back inside. This can be done by hand or by machine.

After the beaded edging is in place, the visible outer threads are colored with permanent marker to approximate the bead color.

Actual-size templates

Trace these actual-size templates on tracing paper; one flap, two bodies, four gussets. Join the parts as shown to create one-piece template about 14.75" x 8" at the widest part.

Leather, non-woven support and Ultrasuede lining are layered, fine-trimmed, basted and then edged together to form the bag. Gussets are joined at the fold line (dotted).

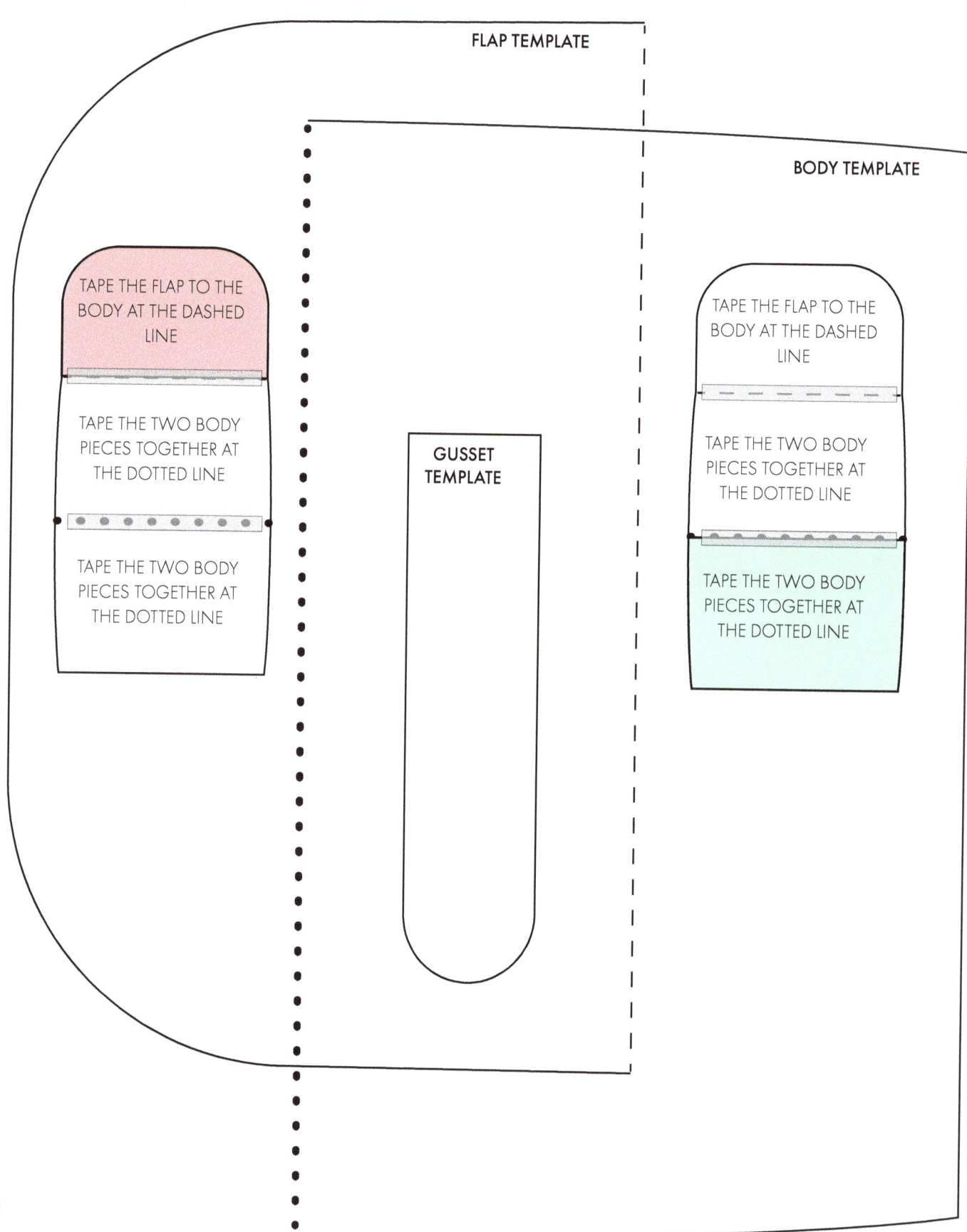

FLAP TEMPLATE

BODY TEMPLATE

TAPE THE FLAP TO THE BODY AT THE DASHED LINE

TAPE THE TWO BODY PIECES TOGETHER AT THE DOTTED LINE

TAPE THE TWO BODY PIECES TOGETHER AT THE DOTTED LINE

GUSSET TEMPLATE

TAPE THE FLAP TO THE BODY AT THE DASHED LINE

TAPE THE TWO BODY PIECES TOGETHER AT THE DOTTED LINE

TAPE THE TWO BODY PIECES TOGETHER AT THE DOTTED LINE

CUT BOTH THE
OUTER SHELL IN
LEATHER AND
THE LINING IN
ULTRASUEDE, BOTH
AT FULL ACTUAL SIZE

TRIM 1/8' ALL AROUND
FROM THE TRACED
TEMPLATE THEN
USE THE TRIMMED
TEMPLATE TO CUT
THE NON-WOVEN
SUPPORT

MARK DOTS ON
INSIDE OF CUT
PIECES TO INDICATE
PLACEMENT OF THE
CENTER BOTTOM
OF GUSSET

MARK DOTS ON
INSIDE OF CUT
PIECE TO INDICATE
THE PLACEMENT
OF THE CENTER
BOTTOM OF
GUSSET

Layer the cut parts with the dots aligned as shown. You'll see immediately that the parts will not align at the short edges. The size determiner should be the leather. The leather will stretch slightly, the non-woven will retain its size, and the Ultrasuede will stretch a lot so take care to avoid stretching.

Baste with a size 10 or 12 glover's needle to avoid making visible holes in the leather. Retain the folds while basting to force the shape. With the basting done, trim away the excess non-woven/Ultrasuede neatly all around.

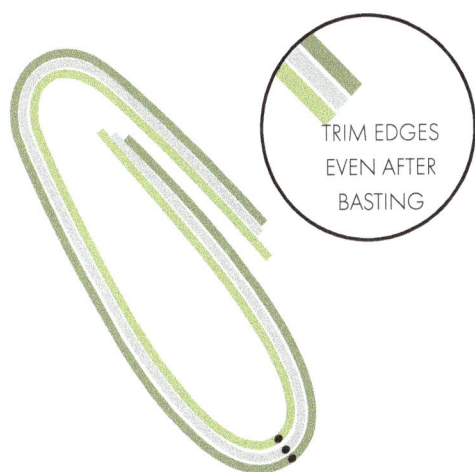

TRIM EDGES
EVEN AFTER
BASTING

CUT TWO GUSSETS EACH FROM
LEATHER AND ULTRASUEDE, DO
NOT LINE WITH NON-WOVEN TO
RETAIN FLEXIBILITY

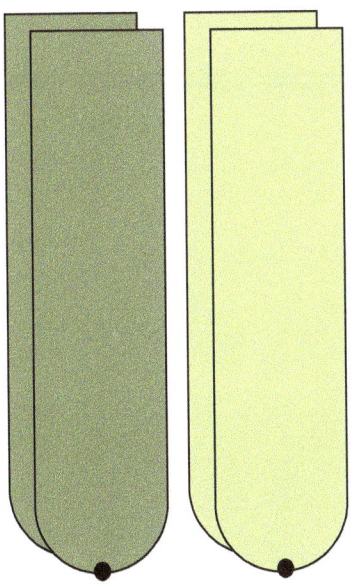

Position the woven strip on the front flap as shown previously. Incorporate it into the basting. Used 4mm heishi as the edging bead at the woven strip's attachment point.

The center bottom of the gussets are aligned to the dot locations on the basted body.

For best results, start at the dotted point and edge upward from those points in both directions (front and back) and on both sides; this will minimize any potential distortion of the bag.

The top of the gusset should be the last part edged with beads. You may have to trim off the gusset to align it to the edge of the body.

51

Weaving leather

Natural leather can be cut into strips of various widths and woven in a similar manner to heavier fibers. This is why I never throw out leather scraps! Natural suede, which is often quite soft, can be used as well but should be cut slightly wider than leather, which has one surface that is stabilized in processing. Ultrasuede (largely polyester in fiber content) can also be used and must also be cut slightly wider than natural leather or suede.

Leather, suede and Ultrasuede will all stretch as you weave. The soft pull is very important when using these materials. Because leather, suede and Ultrasuede have slightly nubby surfaces, they tend to drag on the warp. To counter this, you can use a knitting needle or crochet hook to separate the warps as you weave so the cut strips can be pulled through softly and laid flat on the warp.

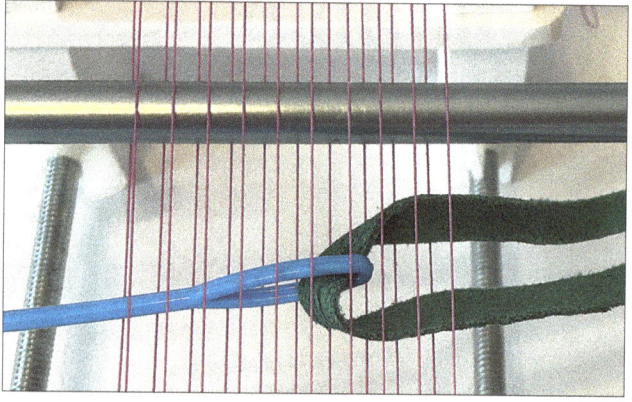

A KNITTING NEEDLE USED AS A "SHEDDING" DEVICE FOR WEAVING LEATHER/SUEDE

Scissors or cutters? Cutting strips by hand yields a pleasingly random result. But if you like things neat use a rotary cutter. Tape the leather flat on a cutting surface and use a ruler to guide your cuts.

Plan in advance for how you will deal with the unwoven ends of your leather strips. If you want an even edge with the end tucked under you'll likely need to add a backing to your piece. You can fold the loose ends under and tack them down to the back of the piece using nylon beading thread and a gloving needle. **Be careful with glovers** as they are designed to slice right through thick, resistant materials (leather), and if you run the chiseled tip of a glover along your warp, it WILL shred.

Another method for taming unwoven leather ends is to **incorporated the ends into your design.** In the little purse on pages 54-55, the leather and suede strips are secured with 15° seed beads to a surface of deerskin. Of course this means you will have back-threads, so an additional backing will be needed to cover those, unless you don't care if they're visible. I DO care, so I usually add a backing of Ultrasuede or leather.

Natural leather and suede cut into 1/8" to 1/4" strips (3-6mm)

Use nylon micro cord in a neutral color to warp the loom; sett is 15 warps per inch. Add 25 warps over a width of about 1 5/8" (4.2 cm). Weave the leather areas first, then work the beading into the areas between the leather strips.

This design is intended to be a bit funky; don't worry about the rows of beads being perfectly level. Embrace the curve; relax and relish the resulting chaos!

About the materials

Use your seed bead leftovers and any ratty old leather you happen to have. You could also use wool rug strips or raffia ribbon in place of the leather!

All of the weaving beads are size 11°. I used Czech beads but Japanese will work equally well.

The leather strips are all about 12" long and 1/8" to 3/16" wide (3-4 mm). At that length you can weave six back-and-forth rows of plain tabby in leather. You'll have enough unwoven end tabs on these strips to fold under and secure with a stitch or two of beading thread.

This magnetic slide clasp is secured through the loops with 15° seed beads in Duracoat gold to match the finish of the clasp. Make a double pass of thread within the 15°s for security.

Scan or photograph and print at actual size of 1.6" x 7.5" (4.1 x 19 cm). Adjust the length as needed, allowing for the clasp you choose.

Sizes 11°, 8° and 6° are randomly added to the edge for decoration; the 6°s and 8°s are all secured with one 15°. The edging serves not only to decorate the bracelet but to hold the suede backing in place. This bracelet does not require non-woven support, as the leather is substantial enough.

This actual size photo can be used as a guide in conjunction with the cartoon on the opposite page. The warping size is 4.125" x 7.75" (10.8 x 27.4cm). Nylon micro cord in a soft lavender-rose color was used. Sett is 11 warps per inch based on the dominant bead size of 8° (one bead between warps) and 15° (two beads between warps). soumak, plain tabby, tabby over two, and pick and pick were used to lay the fibers in place.

Braids created in size 10 perle cotton; three groups of thirty strands each, ten each of three colors matching the leather and bead colors in the weave.

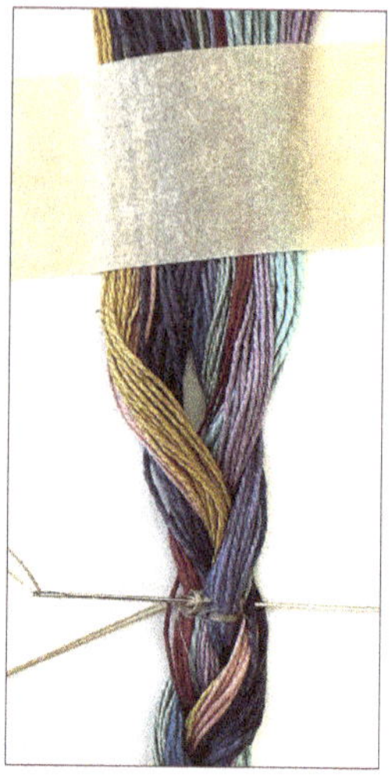

Try to keep the braid flat at the joining point, even though you will be covering the joint.

The leather size of the completed bag is 6" x 7.75" (15.3 x 19.7cm) without the edging in 6° seed beads, which adds about 1/4" (6 mm) overall.

To anchor the unwoven ends of the leather strips, 15° seed beads are used with nylon beading thread and a size 12 glover's needle (careful not to shred the warps!). 15°s are also used within the design as shown at right and add to the overall stability.

Secure the braided fibers together with nylon beading thread and saturate the joint with flexible glue.

This actual size cartoon shows the leather pathways and a few guidelines for adding beads and fibers. Follow the actual size photo on the opposite page in adding woven fiber and bead sections to create your own version of the rectangular panel. Scan or photograph and print at actual size of 4.125" x 7.75" (10.8 x 27.4 cm).

Wipe off excess and secure the braid to the purse symmetrically to the top front edge with invisible stitches; go through the top leather layer and the supporting non-woven.

Five bands of eleven (11) 11° seed beads arched over the joining place and tacked through the upper leather layer

The leather base on which the woven panel is secured is backed with a stabilizer of medium non-woven (pellon 65). After the leather ends are secured, the panel is backed with Ultrasuede. The back of the purse (undecorated) is the same size and construction. The front and back are secured together with basic edging of 6° seed beads; the top edge along the sides and bottom edge; the tops are edged separately.

Alegria

Finished size 16" to 18" necklace

A no-finish loom is recommended. Both sides of the necklace are woven on the loom at the same time.

Thread 8° seed beads onto the warp prior to warping, positioned outside one end of the prongs so that when the work is removed from the loom, the 8°s land at the end of the loom without warp ends. Use size D nylon beading thread or nylon micro cord as warp.

Simple tabby and pick and pick are interspersed with areas of beading. Two buttonholes are added for maximum wearing flexibility. The focal stone is a 23mm crystal triangle bezeled in peyote stitch.

Two weft fibers are used, 10/2 variegated tencel and 10/2 solid color bamboo. Lace weight and fingering weight will work well.

Variegated 10/2 tencel fiber (25 yds)

Teal 10/2 bamboo fiber (10 yds)

23mm crystal triangle

 Delica 416 size 11 cylinders galvanized aqua (114)

 Toho 15° 954 crystal-lined turquoise (208)

 Toho 8° 954 crystal-lined turquoise (87)

 Czech 11° 68506 copper-lined crystal AB (778)

 Toho 11° 165BDF matte transparent aqua AB (452)

 Czech 13° 01740 silk bronze (303)

 3mm crystal bicones deep blue (10)

 3mm crystal bicones honey (14)

 4mm crystal rounds deep blue (10)

 5-6mm freshwater pearls (4)

Before you weave, bezel the 23mm triangle using peyote stitch in the round (appendix).

On a forty-eight inch (48") thread, pick up sixty (60) Delicas. Form a ring by running back through several beads; center the ring on the thread). The ring of beads will fit snugly around the triangle stone.

Add one round of Delicas. Since the initial ring of sixty forms the first TWO rounds, you now have three rounds of Delicas.

RUN THROUGH TWO 15°s

ADD ONE 15° IN EACH OF THE NEXT NINE SPACES

SKIP ONE SPACE

Use 15°s for the next round as in the photo. Start with one 15°s in each of the first five spaces, then *run the thread through TWO 15°s on the previous round, essentially skipping one space. Add one 15° in each of the next nine spaces.* Repeat between *s once more, then end with one 15° in each of the remaining four spaces.

Step 1 continued. Switch to the other thread tail. Add one round of 15°s to the front of the bezel (1G). You will probably need to insert the stone before completing this round. Be sure the "points" of the bezel land on the corners of the triangle stone.

In the next round, use 15°s again. Repeat the round in diagram 1E (shown here in 1H, making sure the two-bead pass-throughs on the front side of the bezel are directly aligned over those on the back (1I).

Now add another round of 15°s, again placing one bead in each skipped space (red dots, 1J). Complete the bezel with one round of Czech 13° 01740 (1K). Do not cut the threads.

1G

1H

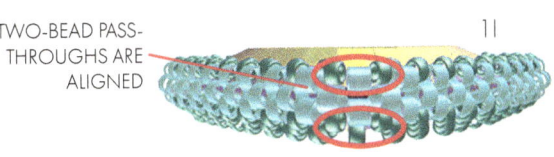

TWO-BEAD PASS-THROUGHS ARE ALIGNED

1I

BACK VIEW

The two remaining threads will be used to attach the triangle bezel to the woven necklace. Weave through the bezel so they emerge from any point on the bezel, in the lowest round of Delicas, in opposite directions.

1J

1K

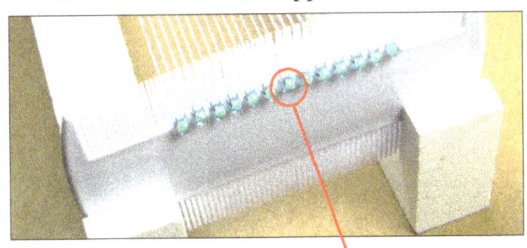

THIS WARP LOOP JOINS THE TWO SIDES OF THE NECKLACE

STEP 2 Warp the loom. This design is woven in two separate strips joined at the center point by one warp loop and further secured by the triangle assembly. Sizing is done at the buttonhole ends; you can adjust the full length of the weave (8.5" recommended) and change how you close the necklace because you can weave up to three buttonholes and use three buttons.

Pull out twelve (12) yards of warp and load thirteen (13) 8°s onto the warp thread. Secure the end of the warp in the outer prongs of one comb leaving a tail of about 5". Wrap the warp around two prongs of the opposite comb, slipping one 8° bead to the outside of the comb before pulling the warp through. At the other end, do not add 8° beads. Continue in this manner until you have twenty-six (26) warp threads; one end of the warp will have thirteen (13) 8°s on the outside of the comb, and the other end will have no beads. Tension your warp if needed and secure loose warp ends.

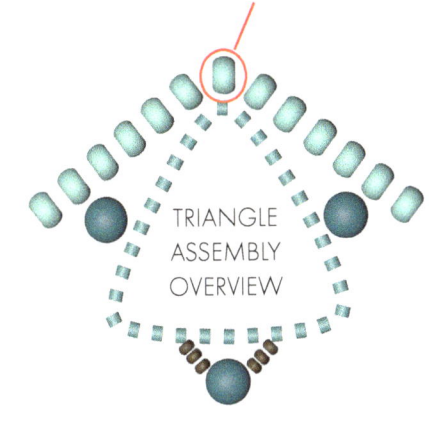

TRIANGLE ASSEMBLY OVERVIEW

THIRTEEN WARP SECTION

STEP 3 Begin weaving one side in basic tabby weave at the end with the 8° beads; loop one variegated thread around the thirteenth warp thread and weave in simple tabby (appendix) until you have twelve (12) rows. Your thread is on the outside of the outermost warp.

Compress the weave against the comb. Weave twelve (12) rows covering only seven threads. Your thread will be at the outer edge of the thirteen-wide warp section. Leave it hanging to secure later.

Loop a teal thread in the eighth warp; weave thirteen rows. Your thread will be at the inside edge of the thirteen-warp section.

Weave across six warps until the added teal section is level with the variegated section, and then weave across the entire thirteen-warp section until you have twelve rows; your thread will be at the outside of the warp.

 Delica 416

 11° 68506

 11° 167BDF

Weave the triangular beaded section, compressing each row as you progress. When complete, bury both thread ends within the beaded area before continuing.

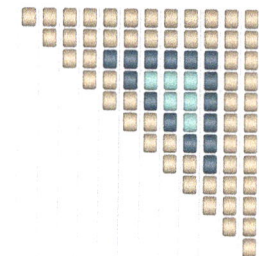

Loop a variegated strand next to the first row of bead weaving. **Weave in tabby** until you the thirteen warp section next to the beaded triangle is filled (two or three fiber rows per beaded row). Weave into the threads that hold the beads to connect the fiber section to the beaded section, then continue three rows past the single bead row, ending with the thread on the inside of the thirteen warp section. This woven triangle will feel less dense than the beaded triangle. Secure and trim the thread.

Weave the next five-row beaded section. Secure and trim the beading threads. Loop a teal thread into the outside of the warp section as shown at the bottom right of the photo in preparation for the next weaving section.

Weave six teal rows in tabby so the thread lands on the outside of the warp.

Loop a variegated thread on the same outside warp, weave one row of variegated and one row of teal, so both ends are on the inside edge of the thirteen-warp section.

Now weave the variegated thread back so the thread is on the outside, followed again by the teal thread. Slip the variegated thread UNDER the teal at both edges to keep the edges neat. Repeat this until you have woven twelve (12) rows of variegated. This is the pick and pick technique.

Compress the pick and pick weave as you progress to form short "bars" of variegated within the teal. End with six rows of teal, secure and trim the thread.

The adjustable button closure

Weave the "stepped" beaded section and secure the beading threads. Loop a variegated thread at the top edge and weave the adjacent stepped section, ending with eight full rows of thread beyond the beaded area.

SHORTENED STEPPED
BEADED ROWS

Loop in a variegated thread and fill the section next to the stepped beaded section using simple tabby weave.

Weave the beaded area with alternating stripes. Secure and trim the beading threads. Loop a variegated strand at the outer right (photo, below) in preparation for the next section.

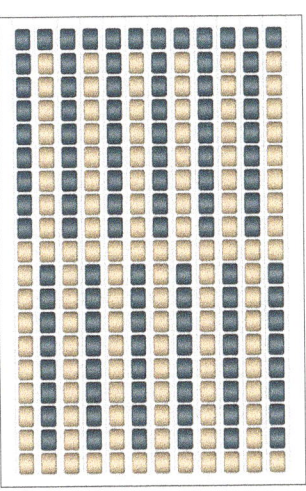
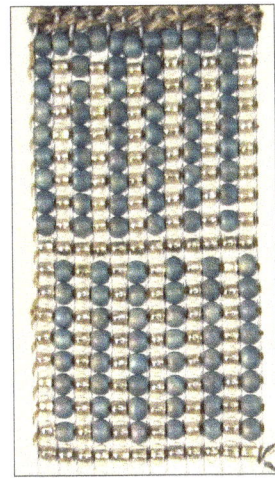

Weave six rows of variegated, then loop in a teal thread and alternate rows to create a striped effect (pick and pick) as you did previously. Weave until there are twelve (12) rows of teal, then finish with six full rows of variegated. Secure and trim the fibers.

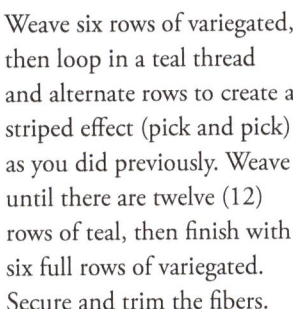

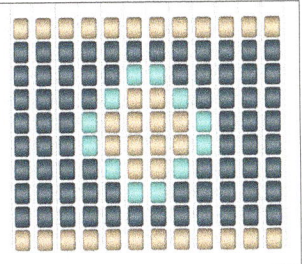

Weave the final beaded section. Secure and trim all the beading threads.

STEP 4 Weave the buttonhole end. Refer to the general buttonhole direction (appendix). If your neck is larger than 16" or you want a looser fit, you can use a loop at the end of the strip to catch the pearl rather than overlapping the ends and using a button. The three buttonholes will only be minimally visible, so if you're unsure—weave them! After trying on the full necklace, you can decide how you want to wear it.

STEP 5 Weave the opposite side in mirror image. Take care not to catch the completed side in your needle as you weave the new side; this is especially easy to do while weaving beads as the needle has a sharp point. Start your loops on the opposite side of the warp section in each weaving area. **Do not weave buttonholes on the second side,** weave the outer section in full rows.

STEP 6 Remove the weave from the loom following manufacturer's directions.. Remove the outer ends first; release the warp thread ends and slide the ends diagonally off the comb prongs. Put a needle on the warp end(s) and run the warp end through the warp loops. Take out the slack but don't pull so hard that the end is distorted. Decompress the weave so the loops disappear, catching the warp end. Optional but recommended: run a very thin line of glue along the outermost edge. It will be covered in beads in finishing.

On the end with beads on the warp loops there will be one unattached 8° between the two sides. Decompress the weave so the warp threads are not visible.

STEP 7 Attach the bezeled triangle to the center area. There are two threads emerging from the center-most Delica round on one point of the triangle. Run both threads through the center 8° in opposite directions and take the slack out of the threads.

BACK

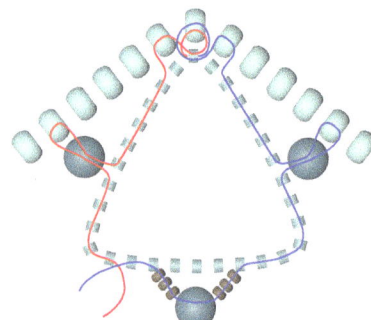

Use both threads that emerge from the center-most Delica to secure the center 8° to the top of the triangle. Weave into the adjacent 8°s, then into the Delica round as diagrammed. Use one pearl on each side to anchor the triangle to the second-to last 8° on both sides. Weave through the bezel to add the pearl, anchored with three 13°s on each side, at the triangle base. Secure the beading thread and trim.

Gabriela

 Japanese 15° metallic gold/silver (652)

 Miyuki 8° metallic gold/ silver (60)

 Miyuki 15° 2075 matte dark denim (377)

 Miyuki 15° 413 opaque medium aqua (378)

 Toho 15° 937 crystal lined orchid (532)

Toho 15° 164 lime AB (379)

 Delica 922 amethyst AB (95)

10/2 perle coton
in four colors

ALSO: 14mm turquoise dyed howlite beads (3); 6mm firepolish round light amethyst; 11° seed bead to anchor 14mm bead (1); nylon beading thread, warping thread, needles.

Warp the loom using size D beading nylon or size heavy mercerized cotton sewing thread. Each side of the design requires fourteen (14) warp threads over about one inch of width. Each section should be woven 8 1/2 to 8 3/4" long.

Weave the left side of the necklace. Begin weaving at the end WITHOUT the two loose warp threads ends. Weave the first section of beads about 1" away from the comb, taking great care not to pierce the warp threads with the tip of the needle.

You may need to run through two or three beads at a time rather than running through all beads at once to accomplish this. Compress the bead rows into a solid area as you progress.

When the bead section is complete, add a fiber section using simple over-under weave (appendix) with a single ply of dark blue cotton.

When the section is 1/2" in compressed length, stop weaving and cut your thread leaving about a 6" tail to weave this in later. Now carefully move the beaded section down the warps until the beads are up against the fiber.

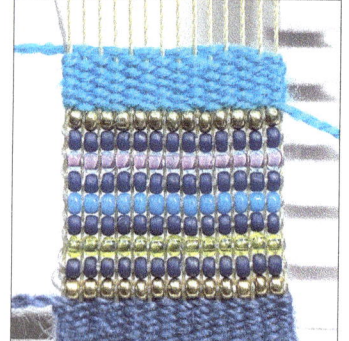

Using peacock blue cotton, weave an eleven row section, starting on the right with a 6" tail, and ending on the left. Don't cut the thread yet, but tuck it aside. Carry the nylon thread upward in the edge of the cotton weave as you progress.

Pick up the seven beads of the bottom row of the next beaded section on the nylon thread, then pass the nylon under the warps. Position the beads in the warps and run the nylon back through them. Add the remaining seven-bead rows in the same manner.

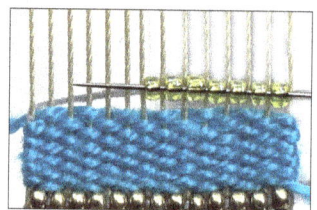  

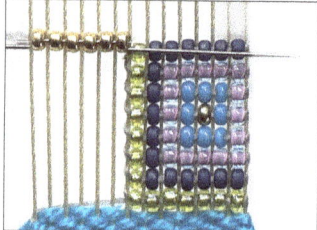 

In the last bead row, which spans the entire width, work the gold beads toward the left, then bring the thread out again at the end of the gold beads and add the green beads in the opposite direction. Secure the thread and trim it.

Fill the open warp area up to the gold row with peacock cotton. Four compressed passes (two in each direction) will fill the distance of one bead. After every four rows, weave into the outermost warp of the bead section to avoid an open span in the weave. When the area is full, bring the thread out on the left side and begin weaving above the gold/green bead row.

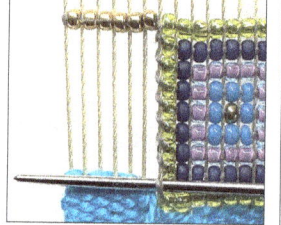 

Use this technique for combining fiber and beads in the same area as you progress through the weaving of the two necklace strands. Four passes of thread, two each direction, will approximate the size of each bead row. Where beads and fiber meet, mitigate open areas by weaving the fiber into the outermost bead warp after every four passes. This technique stabilizes the overall weave and gives greater strength to the completed project.

Weave the rest of the left side, then weave the entire right side of the necklace, following the photo details shown on the next page. The two necklace sides should be the same length. Additional sizing, if needed, can be added between the two back edges of the necklace with the included materials. The friction clasp will land at the FRONT of the necklace.

Remove the weaves from your no-finish loom following the manufacturer's directions. Decompress the weave including adjacent beaded sections until the warp loops disappear within the fibers. Using a toothpick, put a small dab of glue very close to where the initial weaving fiber tail emerges from the end of the weave. Put the fiber tail on a sharp needle and weave the fiber end into the back of the center end.

DAB OF GLUE

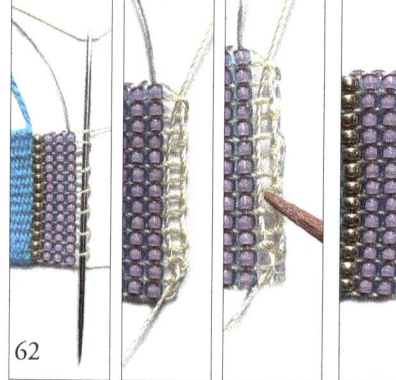

On the back end, remove any securing tape (if you use it) and unwind the two warp ends. Ease the loops off the loom's prongs. If you have nylon thread of at least 10", retain it for use in joining the two parts together. Weave both thread tails through the loops in opposite directions, then run a dab of glue along the outermost edge using a toothpick. Now decompress the beaded area and the adjacent fiber area until the loops pull the end warps against the beads. Allow the glue to dry, then trim the warp tails.

The woven strips are shown actual size, while the graphic patterns are slightly enlarged for more clarity. As you progress, you can compare the printed complete strips to the weave on your loom for comparison and guidance. Slight differences in final appearance are likely, but this will be YOUR necklace, not mine!

Remember that four passes of thread (two in each direction) will approximate one horizontal row of 15°s when compressed. You will have way more than enough cotton thread to complete the design as shown, so feel free to experiment with color sections of thread. You might want to substitute one section of peacock blue in the left strip with orchid fiber instead. Just a suggestion!

Four rows of this dark blue fiber section are not seen as they are inside the beaded strip of peyote stitch

Weave this section at the end of both strips before you complete the adjacent fiber sections. Weave about an inch out from the comb, taking care not to pierce the warps with your needle. Compress the beads against the combs, then complete the fiber section, cramming in as many rows as you can so that when you decompress later, the end loops will be concealed.

In this graphic, work the peacock blue thread first, using four passes (two in each direction) for each "step". Add the beads in shortened rows, then add the orchid fiber section, using four passes (two in each direction) for each bead row.

In this graphic, work the peacock blue thread first, using twelve passes (six in each direction) for the lower section. Add the beads as diagrammed, then the next blue fiber section, mirroring the lower fiber section. Add the remaining beads.

Create the 3D clasp ring using peyote stitch in the round (appendix) using 15° orchid and Delicas on nylon beading thread. The ring will become rigid as you progress and you may find that you need to use a stiffer shorter needle as you complete it. Start with thirty-eight (38) orchid 15°s on a 40" nylon thread. Form a ring by running through the first several beads; center this ring on the thread length (A). Add rounds of the same 15°s until there are five total rounds (B,C). Add two rounds of Delicas (D,E); the ring will flange outward.

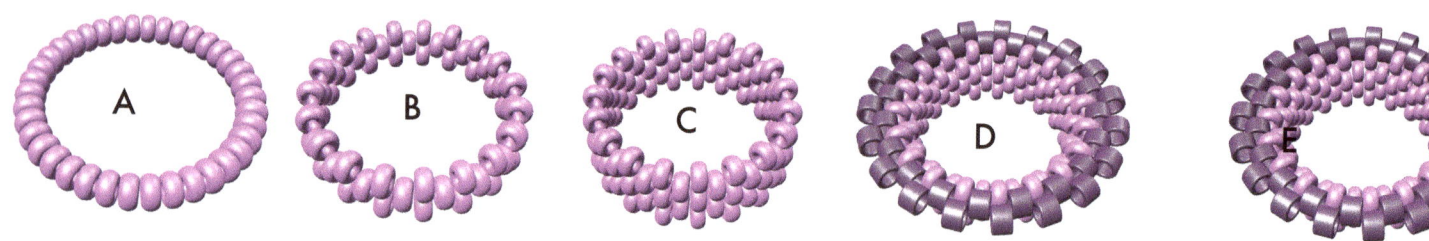

Flip the ring over and add a total of three rounds of Delicas (**F, G**); the ring shapes itself dramatically. Now roll the edges, shown in green and orange in diagram H, and weave them together in a "zipper" fashion to create the 3D ring (I).

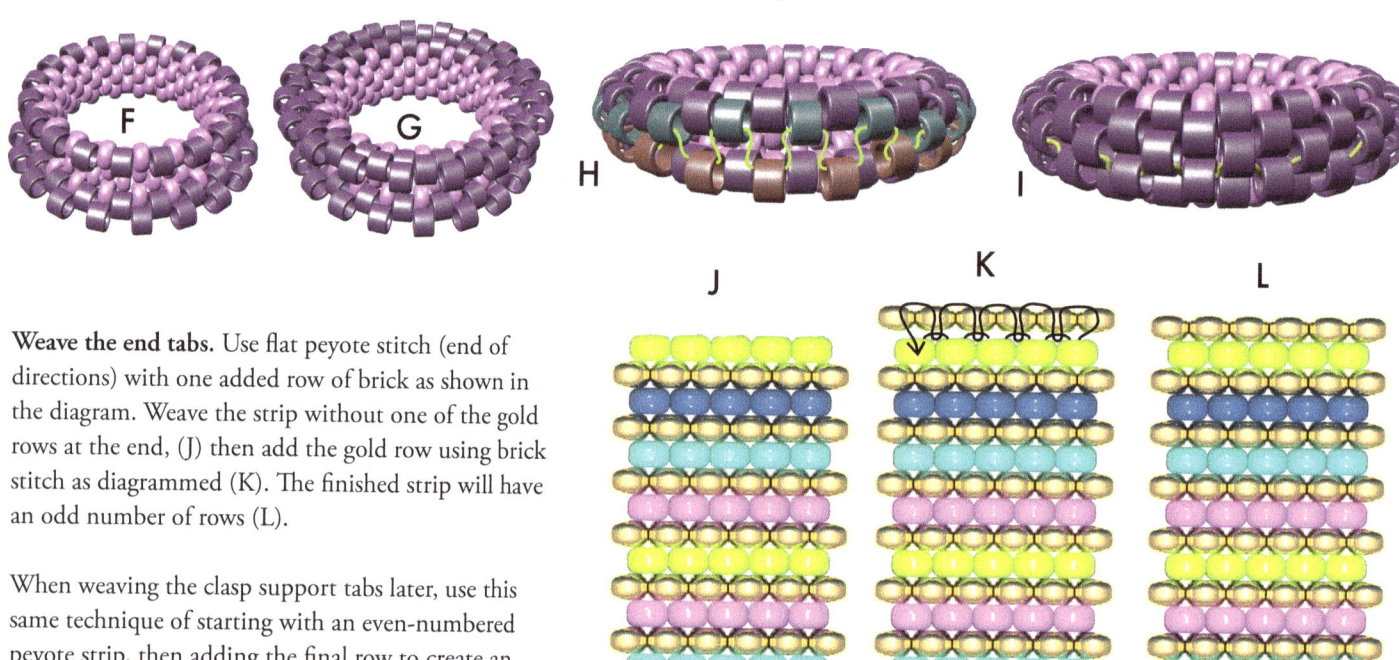

Weave the end tabs. Use flat peyote stitch (end of directions) with one added row of brick as shown in the diagram. Weave the strip without one of the gold rows at the end, (J) then add the gold row using brick stitch as diagrammed (K). The finished strip will have an odd number of rows (L).

When weaving the clasp support tabs later, use this same technique of starting with an even-numbered peyote strip, then adding the final row to create an odd numbered peyote strip. This is infinitely easier and will yield a neater, more attractive result than weaving the entire strip as an odd-numbered strip.

Attach the peyote strips to the center front ends of the necklace. In this photo the needle is shown in red. Roll the flat strip around the center woven edge of each necklace side so the peyote is centered over the edge. Use small stitches to anchor the protruding beads of both front and back edges, keeping the stitches as invisible as possible. Secure and trim the thread.

Weave the clasp tab strips. As with the center end tabs, weave in even-count peyote, then add one row of brick to create two strips of different lengths in odd-count. One strip should have eleven edge beads, the other should have seven edge beads. If you have more than 6" of thread, retain it to attach the strip. If not, secure and trim the thread.

NO BRICK   BRICK ADDED   NO BRICK   BRICK ADDED

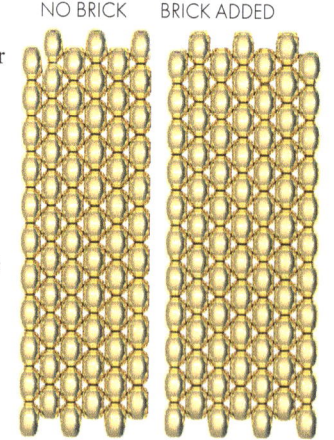

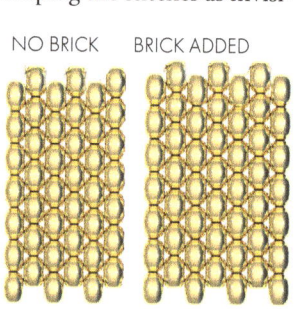

7 EDGE BEADS

11 EDGE BEADS

Attach the tabs to the peyote ends. Determine which side of your woven sides is the back. Clasp tabs are attached to the BACK to give the appearance of emerging from behind the weave. In this diagram the center end strip is shown flat, though you have already rolled and secured it. If needed, secure a new thread by weaving it into the rolled end strip. Fit the protruding beads of the clasp tab into the recesses of the end strip peyote. Secure and trim the thread.

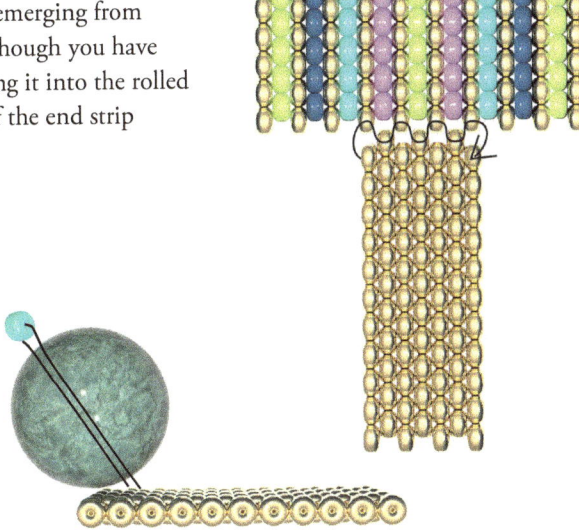

Attach the clasp parts to the tabs. Attach the bead to the shorter tab. Natural stone beads will have slight differences in size; choose the one of your three included beads that fits snugly through the ring, but not so tight that you have to force it. Secure a thread in the longer clasp tab and bring it out of the end of the tab, centered and two beads back from the edge. Anchor the bead with one of the included 11°s. Make a second pass of thread for strength.

WEAVING IN THE THREAD ON BACK

Secure a thread in the shorter tab and bring it out of either side of the outermost edge. Weave the four beads of this outer round into the INNERMOST round of Delicas on the back of the ring. This positioning of the attachment threads will create the appearance of the ring sitting on the tab, as the bead in the other clasp part does. If you have more than 8" of thread length, retain it to add the drop in the next step. Otherwise, secure and trim the thread.

HOW THE FRONT WILL LOOK

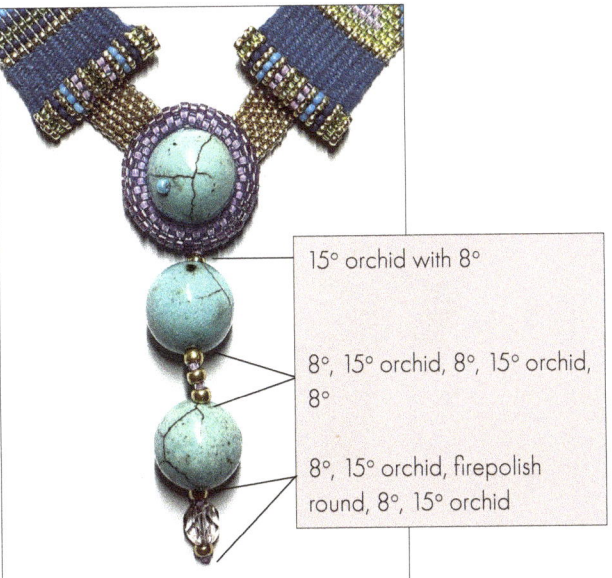

15° orchid with 8°

8°, 15° orchid, 8°, 15° orchid, 8°

8°, 15° orchid, firepolish round, 8°, 15° orchid

Add the drop to the clasp ring. Use the retained thread if you have one; otherwise, secure a thread in the back of the ring and bring it out near the base of the ring (see photo for positioning). Pin or tape the ends of the sides together so you can try on the necklace. Don't worry about the fit yet; you will adjust it when the two sides are joined at the center back. With the clasp in place, note the location of the drop; it should be centered at the base of the clasp ring.

Please note: You may, after joining the two sides, need to adjust the placement of the drop. Its weight is required to keep the clasp in position as the ring itself has almost no weight. You can reuse the same beads; all you will lose is a small bit of thread and a little of your time. This is a true Catch 22! Apologies from the designer.

This is how the clasp will appear from the front.

This is how the clasp will appear from the underside.

Check the fit then join the sides together at the center back. Use a minimum of two 8°s in the joint; three is recommended even if you have no sizing adjustment. This size will fit a small neck (12 to 13 inches). Make sure that the parts are positioned correctly in terms of front and underside. With the clasp closed in the front, try on the unjoined parts. You can pin or tape them together (masking tape only, no duct tape). Use 8°s and 15° peacock for the joining spans. There are enough 8°s to add up to 15 in each span. Secure all but the longest remaining nylon beading thread on either end. Bring the retained thread out of the second-to-last 15° in either end and pick up one 15° peacock, then one 8° and one 15° peacock, as many times as needed to create the desired span, ending with one 15° before attaching to the other side.

Both Muscat and Denim Ice feature 25mm (1")
handmade art mosaic tiles as their focal points. These
tiles are bezeled in peyote stitch, and then attached to
an underlayment of a solidly beaded section. Both are
symmetrical from the center outward. Both are closed
with buttons and loops, and both are decorated with
surface beads, though Muscat is definitely the wild sister.

They're featured together here as there are many
techniques that are common to both, starting with the
bezel, and ending with the closure.

Sister Weaves

Denim Ice materials

 Delica 1208 silver-lined teal (190)

 Matsuno 15° 32 silver-lined light aqua (190)

 Miyuki 15° 2212 transparent pale blue AB (444)

 Toho 15° 82 metallic blue iris (38)

 Toho 15° 998 gold-lined light topaz AB (379)

 Miyuki 15° 52 silver-lined deep teal (114)

 Miyuki 15° 2029 matte light denim blue (414)

 Toho 12° three-cut 540 blue iris-lined crystal (28)

4mm disk beads (12)

 Variegated denim silvered wool

 Size 10 perle cotton deep denim blue

 Size 10 perle cotton light denim blue

Muscat materials

 Delica 1185 matte metallic grape (200)

 Toho 15° 1839 crystal lined light orchid (815)

 Czech 14° 17050 silver-lined gold (40)

 Miyuki 15° 454 purple iris (461)

 Miyuki 15° 411G opaque dyed olive (522)

 Toho 6mm dome (two hole) silk lavender and silk olive (6 each)

 Toho 6mm squares (two hole) silk olive and Picasso purple (6 each)

 Variegated orchid/copper wool, fingering-weight

 Size 10 perle cotton deep purple

 Size 10 perle cotton orchid

 Silken straw olive

Also needed: 25mm square tiles with 5-6mm depth; 5-6mm flat
disk beads for closure.

Warp is nylon beading thread, also used for bead weaving.

Bezel the stone using peyote stitch in the round. The initial round has seventy-six (76) Delicas. Thereafter, use 15° beads as indicated: Denim Ice color/Muscat color

The initial round has seventy-six (76) Delicas.

Add Delica rounds until there are five rounds total.

Add one round of 15° 32/1839

Second round of 15° 32: skip spaces (red dots). The bezel will angle at four points

The bezel will angle at the skipped spaces. In the next round, place one 15° 32/1839 in each space and draw in the thread to further shape the bezel at four corners. Add one round of 15° 2212 to complete the back.

Add one round of 15° 2212/1839 to complete the back

Place the stone wrong side down so the corners of the stone land at the angled corners. The fit will be and should be tight; adjust so corners align. With the stone in place repeat the first two 15° 32 rounds on the front of the stone, aligning the skipped space on the front with the skipped spaces on the back. Use 15° 998/1839 for the third round. The stone will not feel secure until all the 15° rounds are in place. Add one final decorative round of Toho 15° 82/14° 17050, which will draw the bezel in further. Secure the thread but do not trim it; use it in securing the bezel to the weave.

Warp the loom. This design works best on a no-finish loom. Nylon beading thread is used for both warping and weaving. To determine the correct size, measure your wrist and add 1/4" to 1/2" for comfort and closure overlap, depending on how you like your bracelet to fit. Following the loom manufacturer's directions, place twenty-six (26) warp threads for Muscat, or twenty-four (24) for Denim Ice.

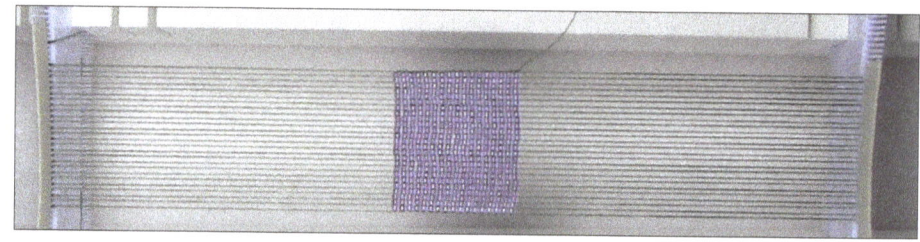

STEP 3 **Weave the beaded center base area.** Use 15° 2212/1839. Add sixteen (16) rows, centered on the warp. If you have leftover thread tails, you can use them later to secure the bezel.

Weave the two sides (Denim Ice). Start with silvered denim fiber. Weave over TWO threads for thirteen (13) rows. Compress the rows dramatically.

Begin the seven-row beaded section. The chart at right shows the full pattern for this section. Start at least one-half inch away from the end of the silvered denim fiber section so you can position one 15° 2029 bead between the warps. It will be difficult to do this close to the fiber with the warps compressed together.

When the first beaded row is complete, push the row against the fiber section and then complete the beads.

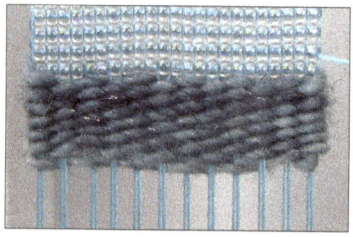

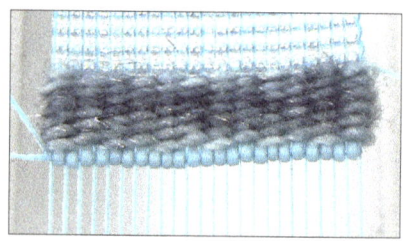

WARPS COMPRESSED TOGETHER BY FIBER WEAVE OVER TWO

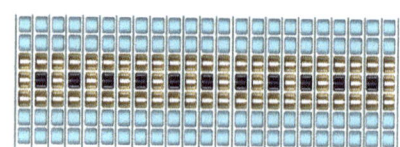

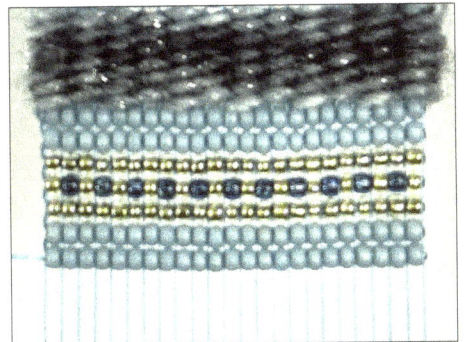

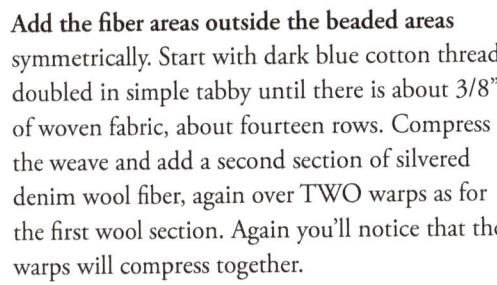

Add the fiber areas outside the beaded areas symmetrically. Start with dark blue cotton thread doubled in simple tabby until there is about 3/8" of woven fabric, about fourteen rows. Compress the weave and add a second section of silvered denim wool fiber, again over TWO warps as for the first wool section. Again you'll notice that the warps will compress together.

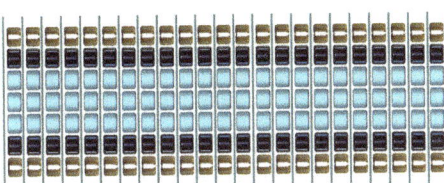

Add the next bead area outside the fiber areas symmetrically. Again, start this section away from the fiber. Compress the beaded section against the wool section.

Weave dark blue cotton outer end areas at the warp's outer ends. As with the previous dark blue section, weave the thread doubled in plain tabby over one warp. Weave a compressed length of one-half inch. If the finished length of the bracelet will be more than eight inches (8") increase this section by 1/8" to 1/4".

Weave the last beaded section adjacent to the dark blue band. Compress this beaded section tightly against the dark blue section.

Complete the weave by filling in doubled light blue cotton. This woven fiber section will vary in length according to how the bracelet was sized. Fill in the open warp gap with as many rows as possible in plain tabby weave. Compress the adjacent rows to "cram" in the rows of weave; buckling will disappear when the weave is removed from the loom.

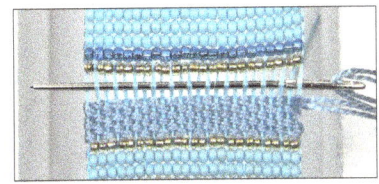

Secure the bezel to the center base. The bezeled stone will just fit into the 16-row center area; secure it by weaving back and forth between the lowest row of Delicas and the outermost center base row. The Delicas will not align perfectly with the 15°s of the base rows, so just weave back and forth as neatly as possible, drawing the thread in as you progress. When one side is secure, repeat the joining on the other side. Secure the thread tails within the center area on the back and trim.

Add the decorative 4mm disks. Using nylon thread, place three disks, each one anchored with one 15° 82, on the inner dark blue woven bands and the light blue woven bands. Space the decorations evenly across the weave.

Weave the thread carefully through the back of the woven areas, keeping it as invisible as possible. Make two passes of thread for security. Secure the excess thread invisibly and trim it.

Weave the two sides (Muscat). The diagrams below and at right show the progression of fibers and beads for the two symmetrical sides.

Use one single strand of silk straw olive in simple tabby weave. The section should measure 3/8" after compression.

One row of 15° 1839
One row alternating 1839 and purple iris
One row of 1839

Work this section last to fill in between beaded sections. Use doubled orchid cotton in simple tabby weave. The section should measure about 1/4" after compression but may be different based on your overall size.

One row of 15° olive
One row alternating olive and 1839
One row of 1839

Start the outer section of tabby in doubled dark purple near the warp. Fill in as densely as possible to cover the warp up to the beaded section.

Seven full rows of olive 15°s

Seven full rows of purple iris 15°s

SOUMAK WEAVE is worked for four rows. Use one strand of silken straw and one strand of dusty orchid wool combined together. Alternate the direction of the stitches in progressive rows to create an angled appearance with the two colors.

Use a single ply of dusty orchid wool over TWO warps; weave a total of nine rows. Secure and trim the tails. Note that the warps will group into pairs; when you start the purple iris 15° section, weave far enough away (without piercing warps) so you can separate the threads.

Compress the beads of the purple iris section up against the wool after the first row. Continue to avoid piercing the warp with the needle so you can more easily compress the weave.

Add the decorative squares and domes. As shown in the diagrams below, attach each bead within the correct location. You can use a doubled strand of thread for strength if desired. Space the beads evenly within each section and secure excess threads within the fibers of beads of the base section.

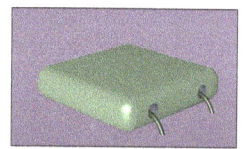
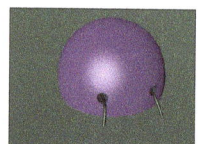

Add the closure. The three buttons are stitched onto the outermost woven bands; the three loops are stitched on the opposite edge of the bracelet. Use twelve (12) 15° 998/454 for each loop; space them as shown, with a slight indent from the outer edge on both sides. Make a second pass of thread through all for strength. On the opposite end, add the buttons in the same manner as for the disks, anchoring each one with a single 15° 998/454. Align the buttons with the loops, and adjust their placement for fit as needed.

Doodling

Weaving without a plan. You start with a few elements based on your notion of what you MIGHT want to create, then just let it flow. What I did plan ahead was for this piece to hang from a 3/8" (1 cm) wood dowel.

The spacing of the warps was based on the width of 6° seed beads, which I wanted to feature and which (conveniently) are roughly twice the width of 11°s. The loom was set up using nylon micro cord with 80 warp threads over 4.75" (12cm), a sett of 16-17 per inch.

The wrap-around band is started with two rows of plain tabby over single warps; this secures the ends of the weave. After the two securing rows, I switched to weaving over two warp threads in tabby to a depth of 1.25" (3cm), so the full length of the warp is 10.75" (27.3cm). Because I wanted to use a bottom-edge fringe, I tied the bottom of each pair of warps together in a square knot (bottom right) and left warp threads of 10" (25cm) to be used later. To keep them out of the way I taped them against the bottom of the loom.

A row of 6°s seed beads, woven over TWO warps, borders the bottom edge of the wrap-around band. This row defines the start of the doodling area.

I started doodling with a curve of 11° beads and an adjacent band of plain tabby, all woven over a single warp. Note in the photo below that the warps are close together in the 6° row and then spread apart at the curved band below. You can join and then separate warps any time, anywhere within the weave.

The curved edge of this band became the template for cutting a pre-painted piece of non-woven (Pellon 65-weight). I held the painted non-woven below the warps and placed a series of dots, which were then used for cutting a curved edge.

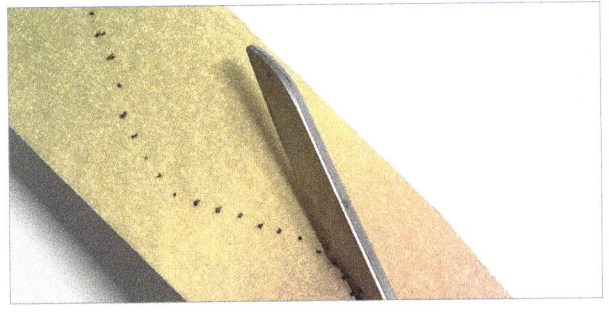

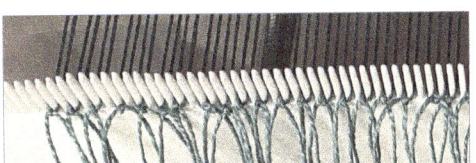

BOTTOM WARPS
TIED IN PAIRS WITH
SQUARE KNOT

71

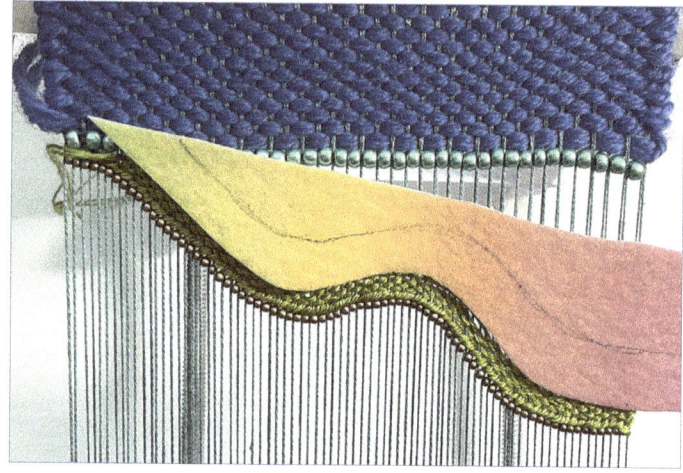

After drawing a parallel curve on the painted non-woven, I trimmed it and inserted it through the warp, using a small plier to guide it. Once this initial curve of non-woven was in place, I painted and cut several more, then inserted them into the warp in what I hoped would be a pleasing manner. Use the actual-size cartoon and the photo of this piece as a guide for cutting and placing the non-wovens if you want to try to replicate them.

Several non-wovens are now in place; weaves of beads/fibers are situated around them to secure them. I used a wood shuttle bar to separate the warps to make it easier to place the warps (bottom of photo). When the shuttle bar is removed, the warps realign to hold the strips more securely. Note how the ends of the non-wovens extend beyond the edge of the warp; decorations will be added later to create an attractive edge.

ALL THE NON-WOVENS IN POSITION

Scan or photograph this actual-size cartoon and use it behind your warps to sketch the curves on your warp. The gradient areas can be filled with painted non-woven, heavy leather, lightweight cardboard or card stock that has been printed with the gradient or painted.

When printing this cartoon from a scan or digital copy, be sure to size it to 4.75" x 9.25" (12 x 23.5cm). The wrapped area of the loom is larger as previously described since the wrapped upper section is included.

Doodles can be an excellent way to use up small amounts of beads and leftover fibers. These materials are the ones I used, but please experiment with the contents of your own stash!

11° seed beads in lustered aqua, metallic raspberry, matte light gold, and opaque olive. Less than 10 grams of each color are needed.

8/2 or 10/2 cotton, tencel, or wool can be used as the weaving fibers. I used six bright jewel-tone colors and often combined them in weaving. Plain tabby, over one warp and also over two warps, was used along with soumak weave. Decorative bands of daisy chain were stitched single-ply and double-ply over previously woven tabby areas.

The section used to wrap around the dowel is woven in three-ply Persian wool; you could also use sport or worsted-weight knitting yarn.

Decorative beads include Japanese size 2 bugle beads, 4mm firepolish rounds and rondelles, 5x5mm Tila beads, 12mm flat disks, and 13x18mm oval beads. These items were stitched onto the woven panel and used as edge decorations. Use beading nylon to sew beads in place. Secure the nylon within "puffy" sections of the weave such as soumak areas to keep it invisible.

6° seed beads are used in metallic copper, metallic aqua (both Miyuki Duracoats) and lined amethyst.

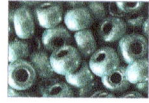

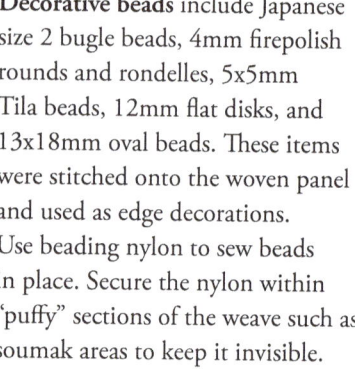

To decorate the ends of the dowel, use a Dremel-type tool or small drill to make a 1/2 deep thin hole in the flat end; use a decorative headpin to secure a 12mm disk over the end.

Glue the headpin and the inside of the disk to the dowel. To start the beaded wrap, glue a doubled thread in the space between the disk and the dowel end before the glue dries. Wrap 11°s around the dowel until it's covered, gluing as you progress, then secure the thread within the weave of the original woven wrap.

The hanging strap should have a doubled thread; use beads from the panel itself to cover the thread. Join the strap to the wrapped beads on the opposite end of the dowel.

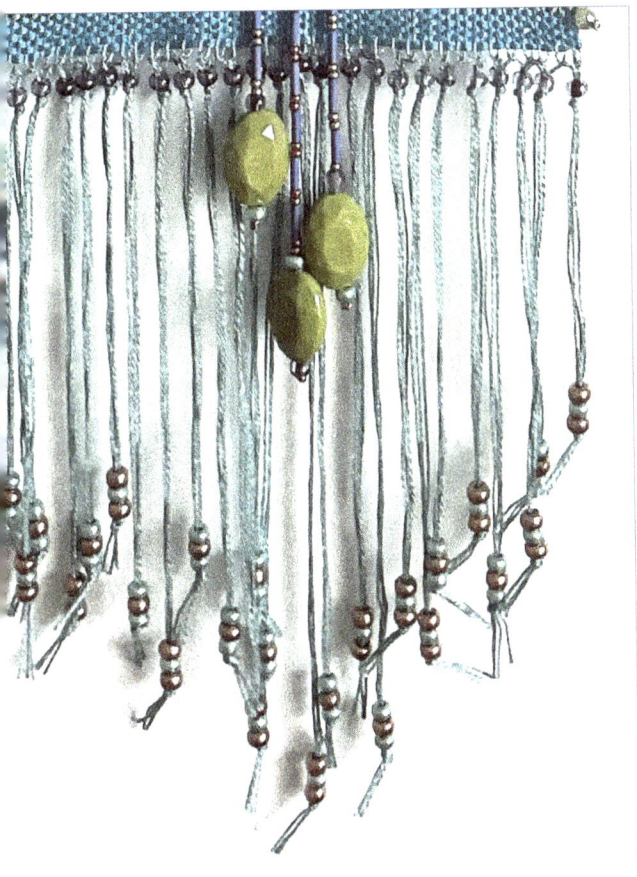

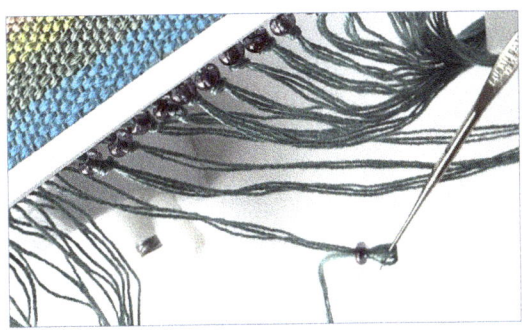

Finish the fringe. Gather two, three or four warp ends together. Using a crochet hook, pull the warp ends through the hole in one 6° (select beads with larger holes) and push the bead up to the edge of the weave. Tie a slip knot to hold it in place. Add groups of three 6°s on each fringe bundle, alternating the ends in a random rough chevron pattern. Tie another slip knot to hold those beads in place, then trim the fringe ends to 1/2" (12mm).

This oversized view of the full doodled hanging panel shows the placement of woven fiber sections and beaded sections, along with the panel decorations and the edge decorations. After the edge decorations are placed, the non-woven strips are trimmed to align better with the decorated edge.

PICK AND PICK USING MULTIPLE COLORS AND A SINGLE COLOR TO CREATE RAINBOW BANDS

CHAIN STITCH WORKED
OVER WOVEN SECTIONS

SOUMAK AND TABBY
ALTERNATING WITHIN ONE
SECTION OF A SINGLE COLOR

SOUMAK WEAVE WITH
MULTIPLE STRANDS IN
COMBINED COLORS

Danube

Warp threads: 26
Sett 13 per inch
Finished width: 2"

The bugle beads are added with stitching after the weave is complete.

There are three buttonholes woven into one end of this strip if you decide to use it as a bracelet. Weave them over 5-8-8-5 warps so the three openings will be evenly spaced. Start with a full tabby strip of about 1/2" before you add the buttonholes.

Straight rows of 11°s are inserted throughout the design as shown. You can carry the beading thread through the fibers at the edge of the weave instead of adding a new thread for each row.

Pick and pick sections should use strongly contrasting colors. Establish one color for a few rows then add the second color. Finish with a few rows of the original color.

Create a stepped weave as a base for the bugles. In one color, start with a few full twenty-six (26) warp rows (an even number), then weave eight rows over nineteen (19) warps, eight rows over fourteen (14) warps, eight rows over eight warps. In the other color, fill in along the stepped sections, then finish with several full rows.

Continue with rows of 11°s spaced by tabby weave and pick and pick as shown.

In the final section weave two colors into each other, with one small area of pick and pick. Change colors and repeat this technique to complete the weave.

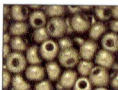 Czech 11° 01710 silk light gold (125 beads)

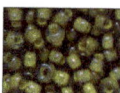 Toho 11° 246 black diamond-lined lime (75 beads)

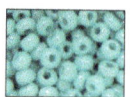 Czech 11° 63130 opaque turquoise (75 beads)

 Czech size 2 bugle 59148M matte black AB (22 beads)

LACE
Jaggerspun Zephyr
50 wool/ 50 silk

LACE
Schachenmayr Tahiti
99 cotton/1 nylon

DK
wool blend

8/2 Tencel
Valley Yarns

DK
wool blend

LACE
70 alpaca/30 silk

Suggestions for use: bookmark, purse handle (repeated on a longer warp), the center strip on a phone case, cuffs on a quilted jacket, wrapped around the top of a small ceramic pot, a key chain

Tasha

1.125" (2.9 cm) x your personal length

This design should be woven on a no-finish loom.

Halcyon 10/2 pearl cotton, light rust (8 yds/m)

Valley Yarns 10/2 pearl cotton Mosstone (18 yds/m)

Valley Yarns 8/2 tencel Straw (14 yds/m)

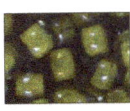 Toho 6° 246 olive lined pale green (up to 20)

 Toho 12° three-cut 303 olive lined brick (up to 375)

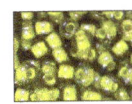 Toho 11° 246 olive lined pale green (up to 110)

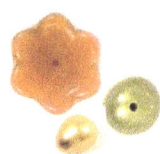 Closure items: 12mm fluted button, 6-7mm freshwater pearl, 5x6mm teardrop pearl

Roughly actual size woven bracelet, sized to fit 6.5" wrist

First, determine the correct size. The actual size photo at right shows the largest possible rendition of the bracelet to fit a wrist up to 8". To determine the correct size for yourself, measure your wrist with the measuring tape directly touching your skin. Add 1 1/4" of additional length, and weave your bracelet to that size. For example, if your wrist measures 6", the total length of the bracelet for a comfortable, attractive fit should be 7 1/4". Use the actual size photo at right for comparison of your progress as you weave.

Warp the loom starting in the center of the weave. Cut a piece that will accommodate your desired length times eighteen, plus an additional 24". You will place the 6º seed beads on the TWO center-most warp threads. Based on your sizing, count how many 6º seed beads are needed. For reference, the photo of the bracelet shown on the previous page fits a 6.25" wrist and has thirteen (13) 6ºs that were added in the warping. Use a fine needle and beading thread to **pull the center of the doubled warp thread through the beads.** Loop the fold point around TWO prongs on the narrower side of the comb. OPTIONAL BUT HIGHLY RECOMMENDED: place a strip of masking tape or a folded sticker over the combs as you warp and as you weave.

With the beads in place, **separate the central warp threads**, then keep looping the continuous **warp thread outward in opposite directions** until there are eight warp threads on both sides of the two beaded warps, for a total of eighteen (18) warp threads, always looping around TWO prongs. The warp should be taught but not so tight that the prongs bend or break. Secure the two warp ends within unused prongs of the comb or tape them securely to the loom brace.

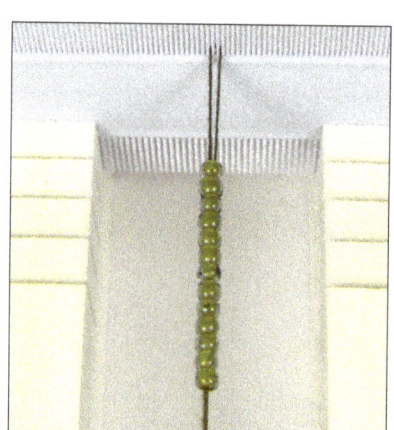

Weave the outermost strip on the buttonhole end. To start, weave a solid section of olive thread the full width of the warp, about 3/8" long, fully compressed to hide the warp. All weaving on the end sections is done in the basic tabby with doubled perle cotton in Mosstone.

Weave the buttonhole. Add two new threads on the left side in the same manner as for the outermost strip, first straw, then olive. Weave pick and pick as follows: work the straw thread within the first nine warps only (dotted red), then, weave the olive row above the straw in the same direction. Reverse direction and add rows, alternating colors in pick and pick.

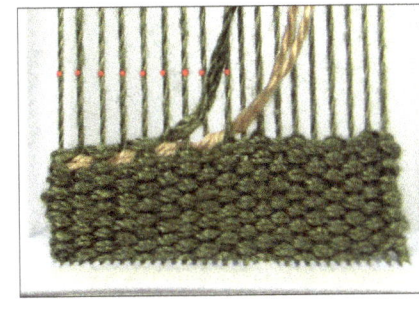

Continue in this manner until the compressed height of the two-color area is 3/4" (about 2cm). You may need to add more thread to complete this area. Secure the thread ends and trim (appendix).

Intertwine the threads on the outer and inner edges of the buttonhole and in any area where colors are alternated by row.

Complete the button by weaving over the other nine warp threads Secure the thread tails and trim.

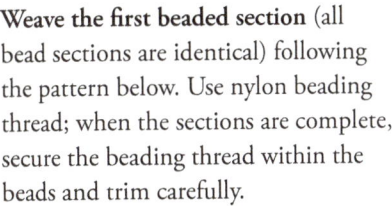

Weave the first beaded section (all bead sections are identical) following the pattern below. Use nylon beading thread; when the sections are complete, secure the beading thread within the beads and trim carefully.

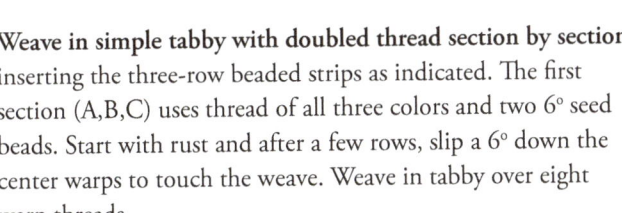

Weave in simple tabby with doubled thread section by section, inserting the three-row beaded strips as indicated. The first section (A,B,C) uses thread of all three colors and two 6° seed beads. Start with rust and after a few rows, slip a 6° down the center warps to touch the weave. Weave in tabby over eight warp threads.

Leave the rust thread out to the side; attach a doubled straw thread on the opposite side. Weave eight warp threads until you fill the area to the right of the bead, then weave completely across the warp for several rounds. Bring another 6° down the center warps, then weave straw to the right of the bead (B).

Leave the straw thread on the right side. Attach an olive thread on the opposite side, and weave eight warps until you reach the top of the bead. Then weave completely across the warps until the result compares to the section as shown in the photo with measuring tapes (C). Refer to the appendix for instructions on how to secure thread ends invisibly within the weave.

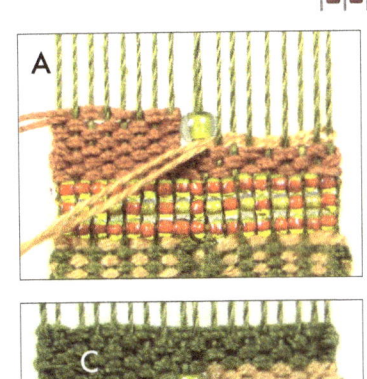

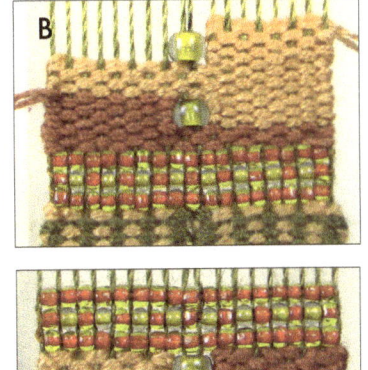
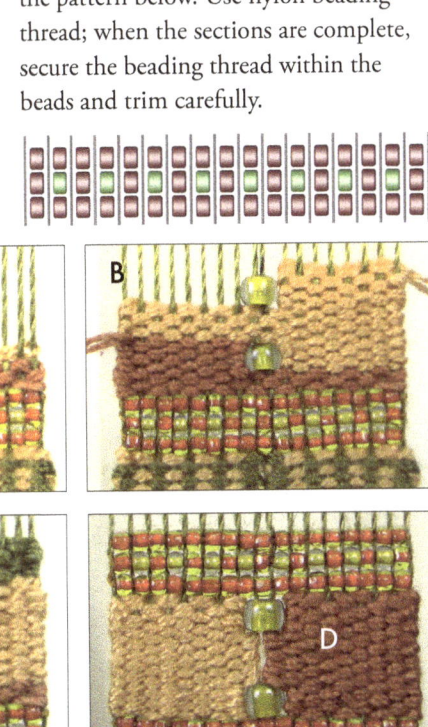

In the next section (D), **bring a 6° down the center warps.** Secure a straw thread at the thread's center fold on the left side and a rust thread on the right side. Weave the straw and rust over and under eight warps until they reach the top of the bead, then weave nine warps, creating a "split" between the two color areas. Again comparing the actual weave to the photo, weave the separate sections. Bring another 6° down the center warps, then weave on both sides of the bead. Secure the threads within their color areas and add a three-row beaded section.

Continue upward, following the photo on the previous page. **Stop adding woven sections and end with a beaded strip** so there is at least 7/8" (2.2 cm) of unbeaded warp.

Finish the weave at the button end. Weave at the outermost end of the bracelet, adding rows of plain tabby with doubled thread, using colors as you like, until the entire end section is tightly packed and the warp threads are all covered. Remove the weave from the loom,

Add the button and decorative pearls. Check the fit of your bracelet and decide where to place the button-flower at the outermost end of the buttonhole. The two pearls are placed after the flower button. Secure a doubled beading thread invisibly in the weave at the button's location; run it back and forth a couple times for strength. Pick up one 11° 246 (choose one with a larger hole), the flower button, and one 6° 246. Reverse direction; skip the 6° and run back through the button and 11°. Reverse direction within the weave and make a second pass through all.

Run through the weave to about 3/8" away from the 11° that supports the button. Pick up one 11° 246, the olive pearl, and one 11° 246. Skip the last 11° and run back through all.

Weave through and bring the thread up about 1/4" away from the 11° that supports the olive pearl. Pick up one 12° three-cut, the drop pearl, and another 12° three-cut. Run back into the weave, then secure the thread within the weave and trim.

Rose Drape

A no-finish pronged loom or rod-end loom can be used for this design.

Warping and weaving are both done with size D beading nylon in a color that coordinates with the overall theme of the design. Each side is warped and woven separately, though you can have them on the loom at the same time. Each side of the necklace requires three yards of thread. The full warp length is 6 5/8" apart, with ten threads spaced over a width just shy of 1". On a pronged loom you'll warp around two prongs, then one, alternating (detail graphic next page) to achieve the correct width.

Fibers

Lace weight satin rayon yarn, two different colors

Hand-dyed 6-ply cotton floss

100% merino wool lace-weight

Beads

 Miyuki Duracoat 8°

 4x2mm turquoise heishi

 Toho 6° 166 amethyst AB

 Czech 8° Terra teal

 Miyuki 11° 2028

 Czech 8° Terra aqua

 Miyuki 8° 410

 Miyuki 8° 414F

 Matsuno 8°

 Miyuki 11° Duracoat

 4x13mm tubes Cape amethyst

 4x13mm tubes amazonite

 10mm faceted amazonite beads

The closure used in this example is a magnetic slide clasp in distressed copper. Sizing adjustments can be made with this type of clasp by lengthening or shortening the loops of beads that secure it to the outer ends of the necklace. Here the loops are very short, but additional 11°s can be added to lengthen them and add length to the necklace.

Warping

Secure one end of the length of warp to the outer/upper end of your loom and put a size 10 or smaller beading needle on the end of the warp. Warping for this design is an exercise in both patience and persistence. You will, I promise, make adjustments as you warp. Before you begin, **cut or rip several 1/2" pieces of masking tape and keep them handy.**

The left interior beads are one turquoise heishi, one cape amethyst tube, and one turquoise heishi. On the right, one 6° amethyst, one amazonite tube, one 6° amethyst. Pick up the first set of interior beads and one Miyuki 8° 410 bead. Wrap the warp thread around bottom prongs or rod so the 8° lands outside the weaving area. **If you are working on a pronged loom, use the diagram below as a suggestion for how to add the warps.** Put a tab of tape over the prongs or rod, then run the needle through the holes in the interior beads in the opposite direction. **Avoid piercing the warp thread with the needle as you run through the beads.**

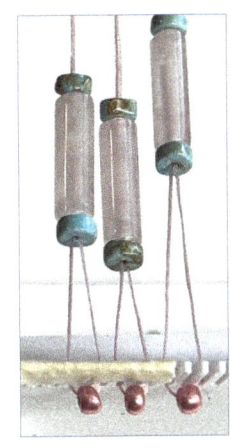

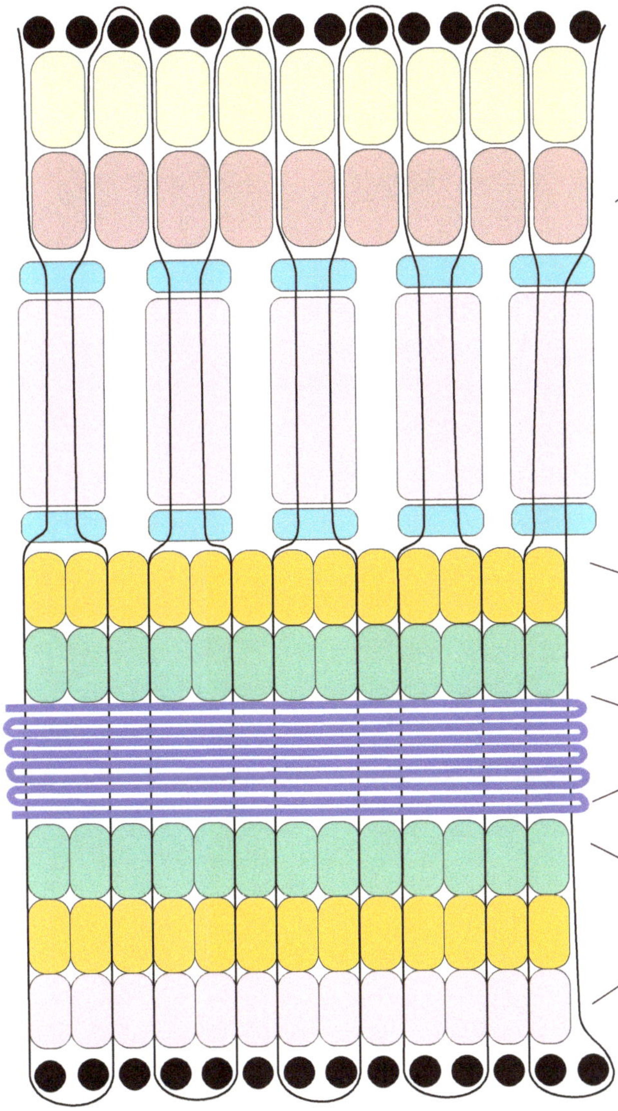

Nine 8° beads woven with one bead between each pair of warps

Note how the warp threads shift when different sized beads are added. Adjusting and grouping warps makes it possible to weave rows of beads that are different sizes.

It appears in the diagram that the edges will be uneven, but **in the actual weave the edges will line up much better, a**nd when the piece is removed from the loom the warp will adjust itself so the edges are nearly even. The two woven strip details on the next page demonstrate this; the variations in the edges are subtle.

Thirteen 11° beads spaced within ten warps

Fiber section in plain tabby or soumak weave

Thirteen 11° beads spaced within ten warps

This diagram does not mimic the actual pattern of weaving for the Rose Drape necklace; use the enlarged photos on the next page as a guide for where to place beads and fibers if you want to precisely replicate the design. **This diagram is intended to show an overview of how grouping and adjusting warps can work to the benefit of your design.**

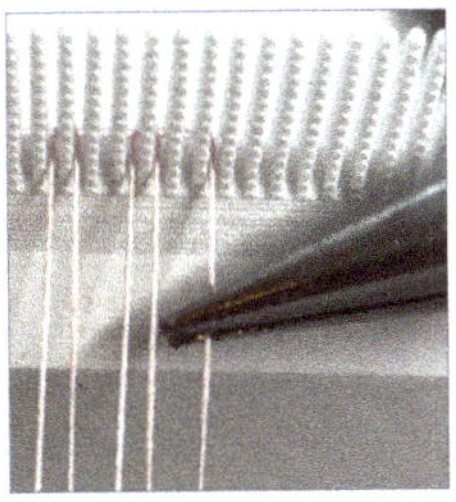

It's unlikely that you'll be able to fully tighten the warp until the entire warp is in place. Masking tape will help keep the warp in place before it's fully tightened. Roughly tighten as you progress, allowing the interior beads to "droop" as you add the remaining warps. You can use a fine-nose plier to adjust the stretch of the warp; if your loom allows it, make final adjustments in the tension of the warp when all the warps are in place.

The two sides of the necklace are shown here fully woven, larger than actual size for clarity. Follow the photograph for guidance in the beading.

Important: in the sections with rows of 11°s, place one 11° between the first two warps, then two 11°s between the second and third warps. Repeat that method across the row, ending with one 11° between the last two warps. Using this method you will place thirteen 11°s across the row; later rows will have nine 8°s in the same width.

The details of the fiber weaves are shown alongside the left side image; the right side is woven with the same dimensions using different colors as shown.

TWENTY WELL-COMPRESSED ROWS OF WOOL FULL STRAND

SIXTEEN WELL-COMPRESSED ROWS OF RAYON FULL STRAND

TWENTY-SIX ROWS OF PLAIN TABBY IN 3-PLIES OF FLOSS

FORTY WELL-COMPRESSED ROWS OF RAYON FULL STRAND

Sizing options: If your neck is average (14-16" circumference) do all sizing in the drapes. Adjust the number of 11° and 8° seed beads in each individual drop starting with the topmost drape and then adjusting the remaining drapes accordingly. If your neck is very small/large, enlarge/reduce the size of the weaving length and add more/fewer rows of 8°s in the outer/upper sections. You can also adjust the closure.

FIVE ROWS OF SOUMAK IN 6-PLY FLOSS FULL STRAND

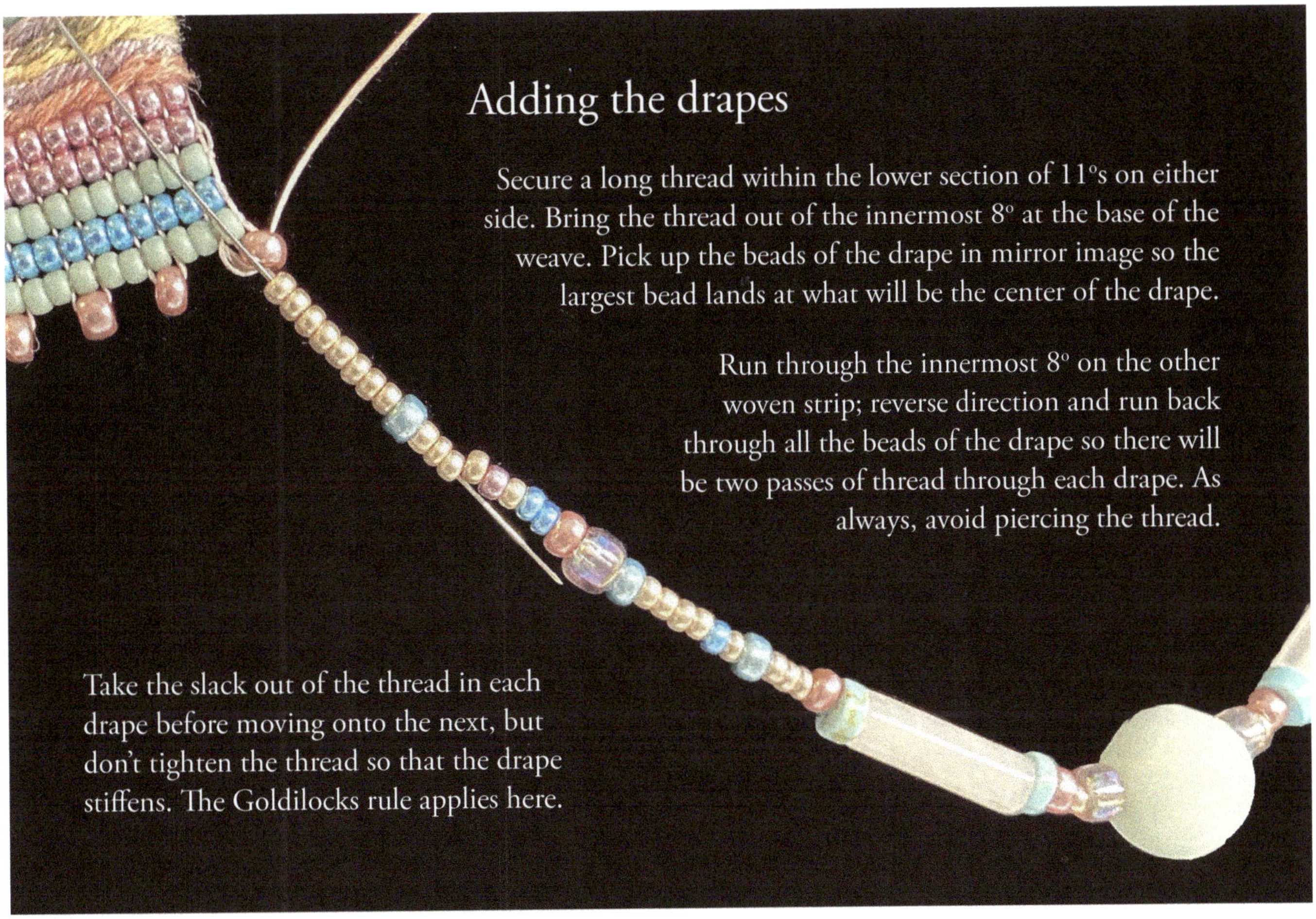

Adding the drapes

Secure a long thread within the lower section of 11°s on either side. Bring the thread out of the innermost 8° at the base of the weave. Pick up the beads of the drape in mirror image so the largest bead lands at what will be the center of the drape.

Run through the innermost 8° on the other woven strip; reverse direction and run back through all the beads of the drape so there will be two passes of thread through each drape. As always, avoid piercing the thread.

Take the slack out of the thread in each drape before moving onto the next, but don't tighten the thread so that the drape stiffens. The Goldilocks rule applies here.

Continue in this manner, weaving into the bottom section of 11°s to move between 8°s at the base of each woven strip. **Make adjustments in the number of 11°s closest to the strip** so the largest beads line up neatly when the necklace is laid out on a flat surface or neck-shaped jewelry stand.

Before adding more drapes than the initial drape, **it's recommended to try on the necklace for sizing purposes.** It's easy enough to adjust the sizing at this point and much harder when you've already added more than one drape.

Neutral Zone

Simple tabby weave over 26 warps is used in this quick-to-make design, which is an example of adding beads to a completed fiber weave. The cotton sections are woven over a single warp, the wool sections over two warps for texture and interest.

You can adjust the EVEN number of warps for a slightly wider or narrower weave.

With a traditional or tapestry loom, use the cut warp ends to add decorations to the closure ends; size D nylon beading thread is a good warp choice as it will go through the decoration beads easily.

This bracelet should fit snugly on the wrist; the back is entirely fiber so it will be comfortable to wear. When sizing, allow 1 1/8" (29mm) for overlap when determining the desired weave length.

 12mm disks (13)

 Toho 11° 51F matte cream (13)

 Miyuki Tila 2035 matte sage iris (20)

 Toho 8° 369 beige-lined crystal (81)

Toho 15° 51F matte cream (81)

Ten neutral colors of 10/2 perle cotton are combined with cream Persian wool. The fibers are I used are mostly leftovers; you only need a few yards of each cotton color. I used nine strands of three-ply Persian wool, each about 1.5 yards/meters for the cream-colored areas; you can substitute an acrylic worsted or bulky weight yarn if wool is problematic for you.

Weave the closure buttonholes and button tabs first using a double three-yard length of perle cotton. Attach cotton lengths by looping around the outermost warp so there is no starting tail. Weave the ending tail into the outer edge of the opposite side. Do this on all cotton sections. Both closure sections should measure 7/8" (22mm) with three buttonholes spaced evenly across the width on one end and no openings on the other.

The buttonholes are spaced evenly across the weave. The two outer sections are over five warps; the two inner sections are over eight warps.

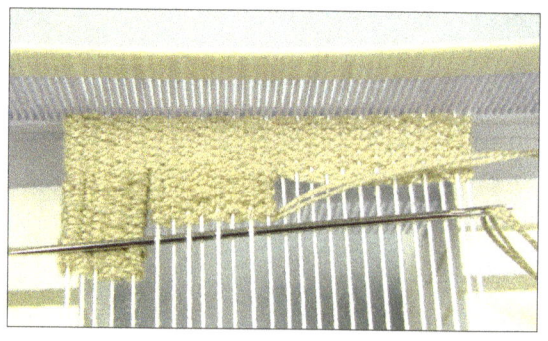

Weaving eight separate sections of perle cotton, each about 3/8" (9-10mm), spaced evenly between the closure ends. A doubled strand of cotton is looped around an outermost warp thread and then woven in simple tabby over single warps. This overview shows the layout of the finished piece with all decorations and buttons in place. You will need to adjust the cotton sections, so avoid piercing the warp.

Each cotton section will later be decorated with the disks and Tila beads. The worsted-weight sections are left undecorated.

Weave the worsted sections over TWO warps and compress each section densely to create texture to contrast the flatter cotton weave sections.. If you're using Persian wool, you can secure each of the three plies separately which will minimize the bulk that is sometimes created in burying weft ends.

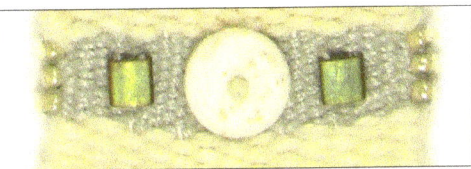

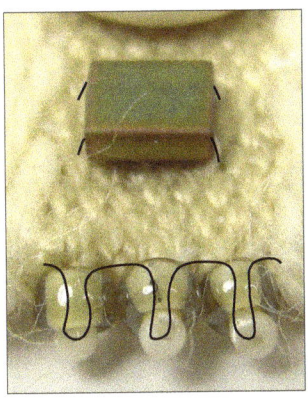

Groups of three 8°s, each secured with one 15°, are spaced around the buttonhole tab in the positions shown here. These decorations add design continuity between the band and the ends.

Add the decorations on each cotton section. Use a light color of beading nylon or ordinary sewing thread to secure the decorations and the three 8° beads added to the cotton section edges. The wool sections do not have any decorations. You can secure the attachment threads invisibly within the back of the wool sections. Disks (including all three buttons) are secured with one 11° and each 8° on the edge is secured with one 15° following the thread path shown.

Poncho Grande

Southwestern colors and motifs on a boot vamp, or use it as a hat band with long decorated warp threads to wrap around the hat's crown.

This design incorporates a number of different weaving techniques in a 1.25" (3.2 cm) wide strip. The rough length on the example shown is 8" (20.3 cm). This length spans the front of my boot at the "bend" point; yours will no doubt be different. The length is adjusted entirely at the outer edges.

Depending on the shape of your boot, the outer ends of the completed strip may need to be folded under.

If you want to permanently adhere the strip to the boot, you will need VERY strong glue, or a large-size (size 6 at the least) gloving needle to sew it in place, and a small plier to pull that fat but VERY sharp needle through the boot material.

Another method is to weave the full strip long enough to create a loop that fits entirely around the boot, a sort of boot "bracelet," and sits close to the heel so the strip does not touch the ground when you are walking. This method allows for cleaning the boot itself without having to protect the woven strip.

Oh, the things we need to consider for fashion!

This strip was worked on a no-finish loom because I planned to use it on a boot and the ends would be visible. But for a hat band, the better method is to use a loom with wrap-around warp, large enough that the circumference of the warp would equal the circumference of your hat PLUS about 8."

This will allow decoration of the warp threads and enough length to tie the ends together. Depending on the shape of your hat, you may want to use double-sided tape to keep the band in place, especially in windy conditions.

Materials

For a boot strap: warp with 30-weight mercerized cotton.

For a hat band: warp with nylon micro-cord.

Sett is 22 warps over 1.375" (3.5cm)

Size D beading nylon for weaving the beads on the warps and adding decorations on the weaves.

The finished weave is decorated with 25 x 18mm brownstone jasper bead, 10mm fluted copper spacer, 14mm round turquoise disk, and 5-6mm turquoise round bead

 JP bugle size 1 Miyuki 2405FR

 Size 11 cylinder Delica 261

 Size 11 cylinder Delica 798

 Size 11 cylinder Delica 312

 3mm glass pearls, dark brown

 Toho 15° 369 beige-lined crystal

16/2 cottolin beige

8/2 tencel khaki

8/2 tencel dark teal

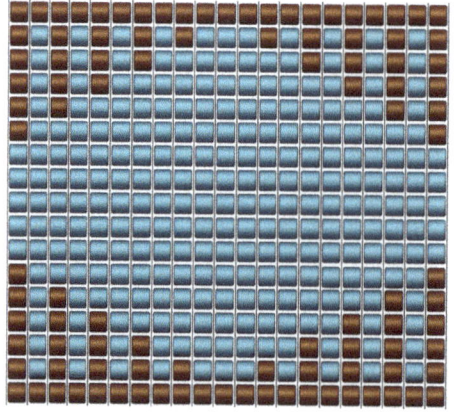

This beaded section is added at the center of the warp length and areas of beads and fibers are worked out-ward symmetrically.

Weave three rows of beads in this pattern.

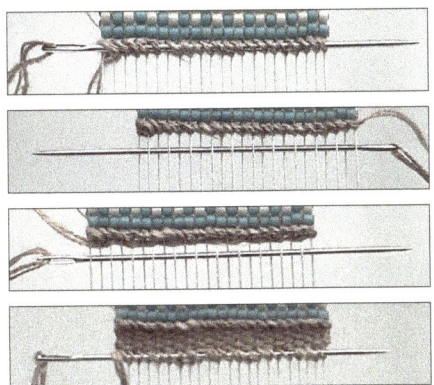

Weave four rows of beads in this pattern.

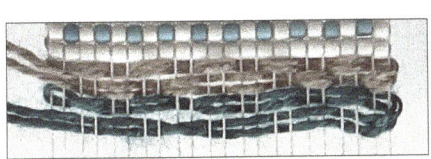

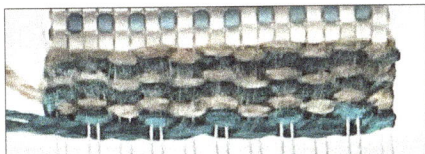

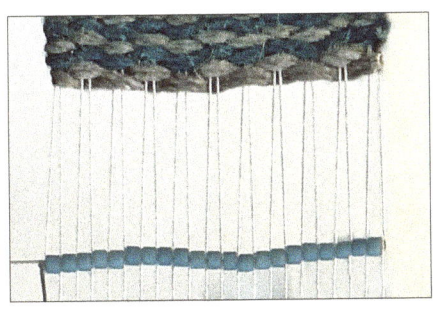

Add one row of soumak (cottolin, doubled); at the end of the row, run the thread back through the entire row to plump up the weave and create dimension. Secure and cut the thread.

After the bead section, start with **one row of soumak with cottolin doubled.** Run back through the row in the FRONT channel to plump it.

Continue with plain tabby over one until there are six rows.

Finish with one row of soumak, and plump it in the same manner as for the first row.

Loop on a doubled thread of toast tencel. The wavy line section is woven over two warps. Start with two rows of tabby over two using a double strand of this fiber.

Loop on a doubled thread of teal tencel; weave two rows of teal in tabby over two.

Compress the weave and continue in this manner, weaving two rows of each color over two warps in tabby. As the weave develops, the wavy line will appear. Continue until the wavy line section has six waves of toast and five waves of teal, ending with the sixth wave of toast.

Weaving over two warps will group warps into eleven pairs. Start the next bead section outward at least 1/2" (12mm) so you can position the beads between single warps. When the beaded row is complete, use a beating device to position the beads tightly against the wavy line section and complete the five row bead section.

LARGER THAN ACTUAL SIZE

Add another SOUMAK/single tabby section in doubled cottolin as previously described, then add the four-row beaded section show below.

93

Using a double strand of Tencel in khaki, **add one row of chain stitch**, working each stitch over three warps. Start by looping the thread around the outermost warp, and place seven chain stitches evenly over the warp span. You can work in either direction.

Add the final beaded section of five rows.

The outer weave section is woven in plain tabby over single warps in a doubled strand of teal Tencel. Depending on your desired length, you'll probably need more than one strand. Secure a copper spacer in the center of the end weave, using a single pearl as an anchor. Make multiple passes of thread for security and positioning.

Edge pearls are added in the beaded sections only. Space them two rows apart. Anchor each pearl with one 15° seed bead. Alternate the depth of the threads as shown above to prevent threads from lumping together within the bead rows.

The bugle beads are spaced evenly over the width of the soumak/tabby section. Adjust the size of the section if needed so the bugles just touch the SOUMAK weave on both open ends of the bugle. Use two passes of thread, both for security and for the ability to position the bugle just so.

Add the teardrop shaped stone first, securing it within the two center-most rows of beads. Use multiple passes of thread for strength and positioning. When secure, bring the thread out of either end and add the 6mm round anchored with one 15°. Secure any excess threads within the beaded area and trim.

Using a charted design with fibers

You can work fibers into sections of charted designs intended for only beads in plain tabby. The beads should be added first as you progress through the weave; depending on the weight of your fiber, you will likely need multiple passes of fiber alongside each bead. In this example the lines of fiber weave are shown as continuous threads over the chart; in reality the fibers will go over and under the warps.

FIBERS WORKED IN
PLACE OF BEADS IN
THESE SECTIONS

Shown side by side, you can see where fibers might be used in a fully charted design. It's a good practice to work the threads mostly over three or more warps; at the very edges, you may be working over only two. The fibers reach into the warps adjacent to the beads as previously described.

Concita

Poncho's little sister.

A no-finish loom is recommended.

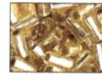 Japanese size 1 bugles silver-lined gold (96)

 Toho 15° hex beads 84 matte dark bronze (378)

 Toho 15° hex beads 25 opaque cream (254)

 Miyuki 15° hex beads 412 opaque turquoise (512)

Miyuki 15° seed beads silver-lined gold (76)

20 x 15 mm turquoise puffy ellipse focal bead

11° seed beads matte metallic chocolate (8)

 8/2 Perle cotton
or tencel, cream
12 yds/meters

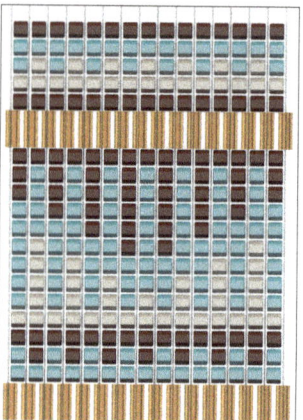

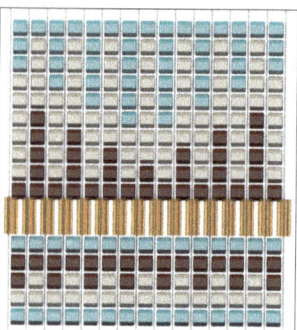

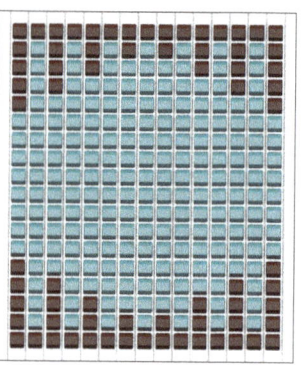

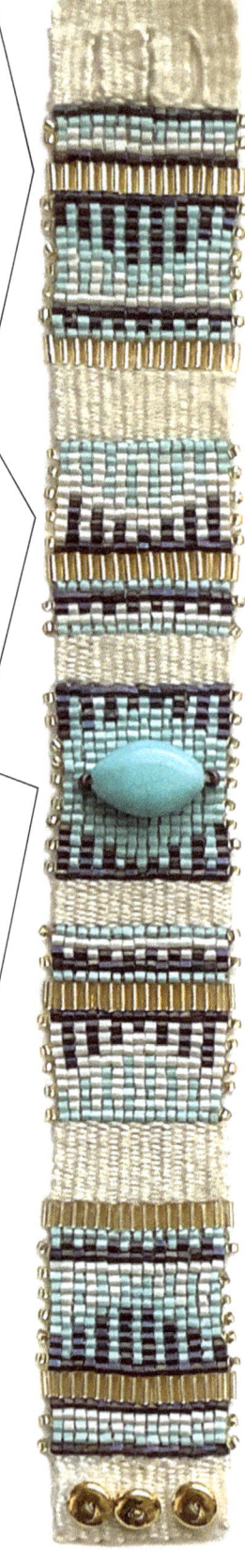

Size D beading nylon warp with the 96 silver-lined gold
bugle beads preloaded; 5-6mm disks for the closure; 11°
seed beads to anchor the closure and the focal bead

Measure your wrist, size the loom for a close fit,
allowing a i/2" overlap for the buttons.

Position all of the bugle beads on the center of the warp
length to keep them temporarily out of the way.

Start weaving at either end of the warp; **weave 12 rows of
single ply fiber in plain tabby.** Compress the weave against
the end of the warp.

Following the directions for buttonholes (appendix) **weave a
3/8" section of buttonholes spaced at the 1/4, 1/2, and 3/4
positions** over the width of the weave. Compress, then set the
weaving thread aside to be secured later.

At the other end, **weave a 1/2" well-compressed section**
of plain tabby, single ply, on which you will later sew the
buttons.

Weave the outermost beaded section in its entirety,
positioning the bugles in two rows across the span of the warp
as shown in the diagram. Take special care not to pierce the
warp threads as you may need to adjust the positions of the
beaded section. Secure and trim the beading thread.

Weave the second bead section as
shown in the diagram, again taking care
not to pierce the warp. Secure and trim
the beading thread.

Weave the central beaded section as
diagrammed.

Mirror the other two beaded sections
and weave them as diagrammed; see the
photo for the mirrored view.

SHOWN LARGER
THAN ACTUAL SIZE

BUTTONHOLES

FIRST BEADED SECTION

SECOND BEADED SECTION

CENTER BEADED SECTION

The focal bead is secured with
11°s on both ends to hide the
beading thread

SECOND BEADED SECTION

Mirrored vertically

FIRST BEADED SECTION

Mirrored vertically

BUTTON TAB

1/2" of plain tabby in
single ply fiver

Position the beaded sections roughly as shown in the
photo. The outer beaded sections should be compressed
against the buttonhole and tab sections at the ends of the
weave.

Weave plain tabby in single ply fiber between the beaded
sections, well compressed, so the resulting bracelet weave is
roughly symmetrical.

Remove the woven strip from the loom and secure any
excess fibers or beading threads.

Secure a doubled beading thread in the tab end. Position
the three buttons so they are aligned with the buttonholes.
**For each button, pick up one 11°, the disk and another
11°.** Skip the outer 11° and run back through the disk
and the first 11°. Run into the weave as if it was fabric
and take the slack out of the beading thread so the button
sits neatly against the tab. Repeat this with the other two
buttons, then secure the beading thread within the tab and
trim it.

Secure a single beading thread within the outer row of the
outermost beaded section. **Add single bead decorations of
silver-lined gold 15°s** as shown in the photo, spacing them
on every other row in the beaded sections only.

When you reach the center beaded section, stitch the
ellipse bead in place on the center bead section with one
11° at each end to hide the beading thread. Make two
passes of thread for strength.

**Continue in this manner until the decorations are all
in place** on both edges. A second beading thread may be
needed.

97

A Case of You

Fits a lot of phones!

10/2 perle cotton
10 yd/m

Sport weight Snuggly
Bamboo/cotton 6 yd/m

Fingering weight silk/wool
variegated

Fingering weight Zooey
cotton/linen blend 20
yd/m

Fingering weight Koigu
merino wool variegated
20 yd/m

DMC metallic six-ply floss
one hank

 Miyuki size 1 bugle 2405 (181)

 Miyuki 11° 2028 (151)

 Toho 11° 995 (584)

 Toho 11° 1611 (758)

Add thirty-four (34) warps at 13 sett for a rough width of about 2.7" (6.9 cm)

C-lon Micro Cord warp

This design is symmetrical, mirrored from the vertical center.

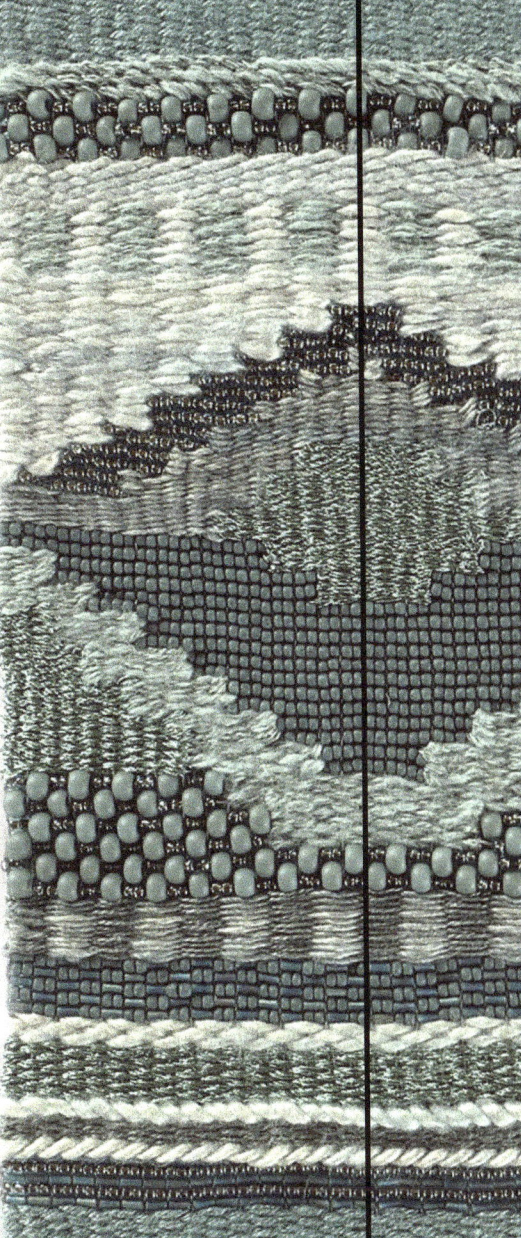

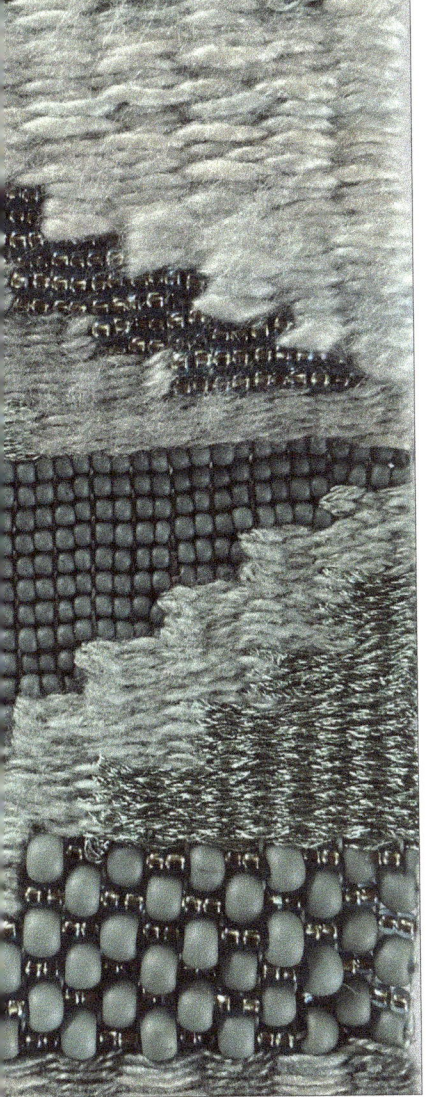

Seventeen rows bamboo/cotton plain weave

Three rows linen/cotton in soumak, all same direction

Three rows alternating 6° with two 11°. Alternate starting beads for honeycomb effect

Nine rows Weight 3 plain weave

Six rows pick and pick with Zooey and Weight 3

Four rows Weight 3 plain weave on TWO warps.

Seven four-row stepped sections of Weight 3 in plain weave over TWO in which two warps are dropped after each section, diminishing to the outer edge over about 1" (2.5cm) of length

Toho 11° 995 in stepped four-row sections aligned with the previous Weight 3 stepped section

Stepped section with seven steps of plain weave in Koigu aligned with the 11° section above it

Stepped section of Toho 11° 1611 dropping/adding two warps to form a void below the Koigu section

Void filled with plain weave using DMC metallic floss

Six rows alternating 6° with two 11°. Alternate starting beads for honeycomb effect

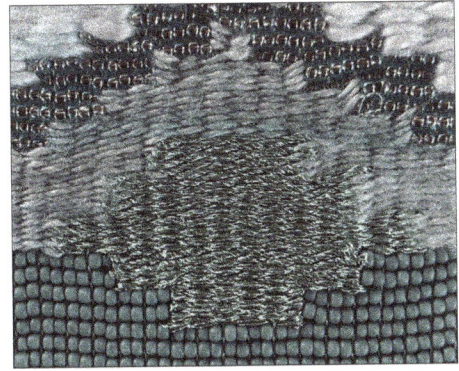

Weave into the warps of the beaded sections to create a solid fill of fiber in sections where beads and fibers join

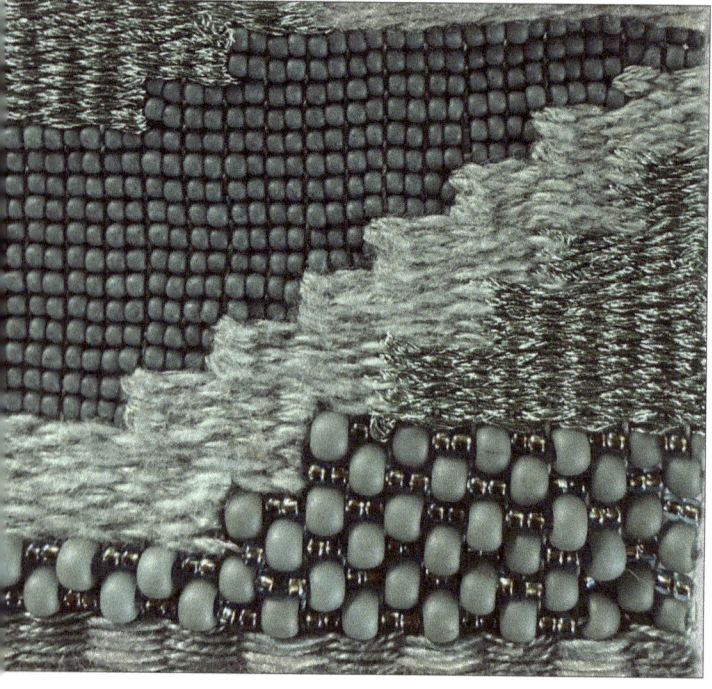

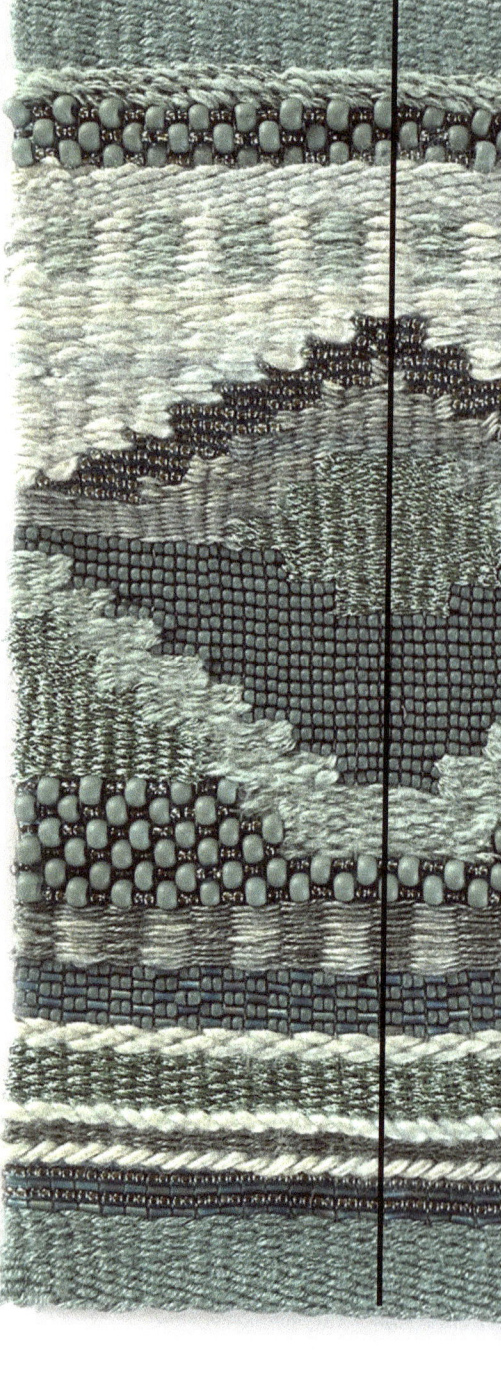

Four-row stepped sections of Zooey in plain weave aligned to the base of the 11° section

Six rows alternating 6° with two 11° aligned to the lowest two steps of Zooey..

Pick and pick over two warps with DOUBLED perle cotton and Koigu.

Five rows alternating 11° and bugles

Three rows plain tabby in Weight 3

Eleven rows plain weave in DMC metallic floss

One row soumak in weight 3, six rows plain weave in 10/2 cotton DOUBLED, one row soumak in the opposite direction in Weight 3

Alternating rows of bugles and 11° 995 over five rows

Seventeen rows bamboo/cotton plain weave

Woodstock

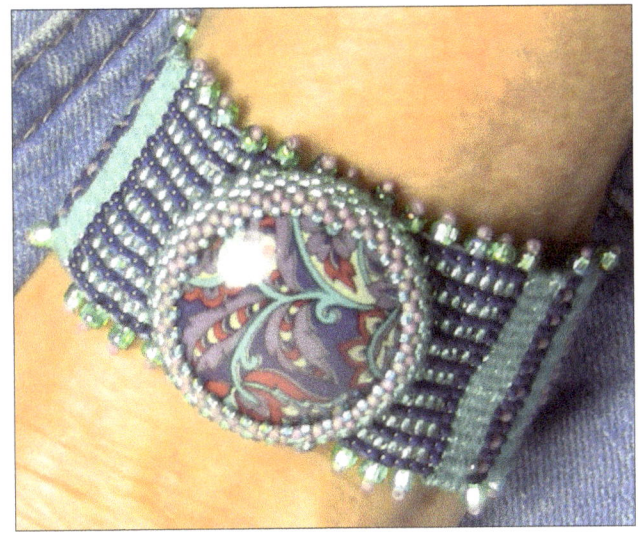

 Czech 11° 02040M matte light amethyst (448)

 Czech 11° 33070 opaque deepest blue (383)

 Czech 11° BL1291 silver-lined aqua (550)

 Toho 15° 1634F matte lavender AB (227)

 Matsuno 8° 645 silver-lined teal AB A(50)

 Miyuki 15° 645 silver-lined teal AB (35)

ALSO: 30mm round vintage resin paisley cabochon; 6-7mm genuine freshwater pearls (2)); warping thread and nylon beading thread; beading and weaving needles

 Deep royal blue wool (4 yds)

 Size 8/2 tencel grayed teal (6 yds)

 Gutermann metallic ice aqua (2 yds)

Bezel the stone. Use peyote stitch in the round (if you're unfamiliar, there is a tutorial at the end of these directions). Cut a nylon thread about 50" long. Pick up seventy (70) 11° BL1291; form a ring by running through several beads; center the ring on the thread length. The ring will fit neatly around the cabochon. Add 11° rounds until there are four rounds total. Add two rounds of 15° 1634F, drawing in the thread to shape the bezel as you progress. Add one round of 15° 645 and secure the thread. Place the bezel over the front of the stone. Secure and trim this thread end, then put the needle on the other thread end.

Invert the assembly and add two complete rounds of 15° 1634F, again drawing in the thread as you progress. Add one final round of 15° 1634F, but skip spaces (red dots) to reduce the number of beads from 35 to 29. Drawing in the thread to tighten the bezel as you progress. The fit will and should be tight. Secure the thread but if there's more than eight inches left, do not cut it; you'll use it to secure the bezeled stone to the woven bracelet later.

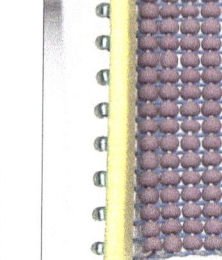

Warp the loom with nylon beading thread; put a needle on one end. Load seventeen (17) 11° 1291 onto the thread. To determine the correct size, measure your wrist and add 3/4" to 1" for comfort and closure overlap. Measure between slots on the loom to determine which slots will give the closest length (deferring to slightly larger rather than smaller). Secure the warp thread to one end leaving tail of about 7". Set the loom combs into those slots with the side for 11s facing up. Following the loom's directions, place eighteen (18) warp threads. As you loop each thread around the prongs, place one 11° OUTSIDE the weaving area; these beads will be incorporated into the finishing later.

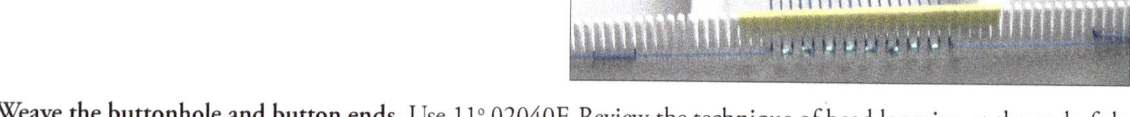

Weave the buttonhole and button ends. Use 11° 02040F. Review the technique of bead looming at the end of these directions. Start slightly away from the prongs; you'll shift the rows later. Add three complete rows and five short rows over six warps (five beads). Add two complete rows, then rotate the loom and add five short rows on the other side. Push the section to the prongs and weave through the rows so you can fill in the center area with five short rows, leaving two buttonhole spaces as shown. Secure and trim the thread. On the opposite end, weave ten full rows of 11°s and

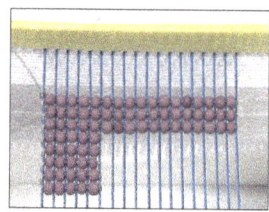

compress the weave against the prongs. Pearls will later be added to the full-row section to form the closure.

Continue with fiber and beaded sections. As always, TAKING CARE NOT TO PIERCE THE WARP THREADS so you can compress the weave later. The two sides are symmetrical beyond the buttonhole/pearl ends.

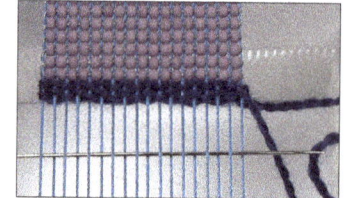

Start with a full strand of dark blue wool. Leaving a 3" tail which you will catch in the weave as you progress, weave in simple over-under as described in the tutorial at the end of these directions until the section is about 1/4" long when well compressed. NOTE: If your wrist s large (7.75"+) add two more rows in all wool sections for sizing. End with the thread on the left side. Run the end of the thread through the outermost fibers to secure it and trim carefully, taking care not to cut the warps.

BEST PRACTICE TIP: Catch the starting tail within the weave on the outer edge, then trim it later, taking care not to cut warps

Add bead section 1, a second dark blue wool section, and bead section 2. Compress all fully toward the prongs. The tencel section that follows will begin with one row of simple over-under, but will continue in a different weave (next page).

BEAD SECTION 1

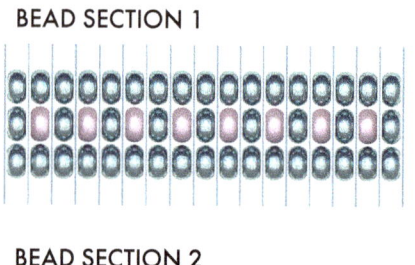

BEAD SECTION 2

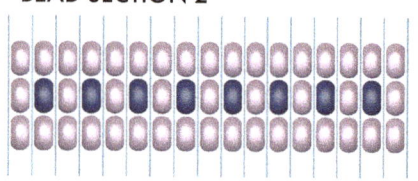

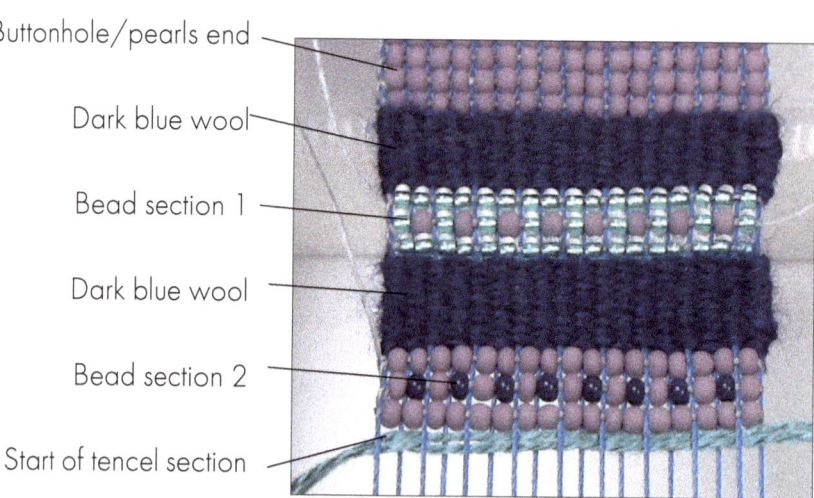

Buttonhole/pearls end

Dark blue wool

Bead section 1

Dark blue wool

Bead section 2

Start of tencel section

Combine two tencel strands and begin the next section with one row of plain tabby. Weave over TWO warp threads as shown in the photos; as you progress, a distinctly raised texture will result. Continue weaving over two warps until you have about 6" remaining and the thread is on the left. Secure the thread and trim it. Compress the weave.

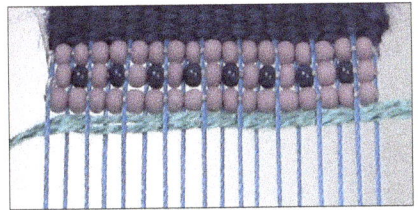
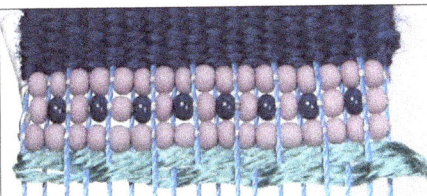
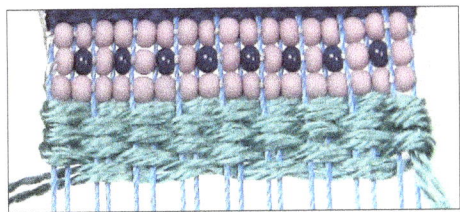

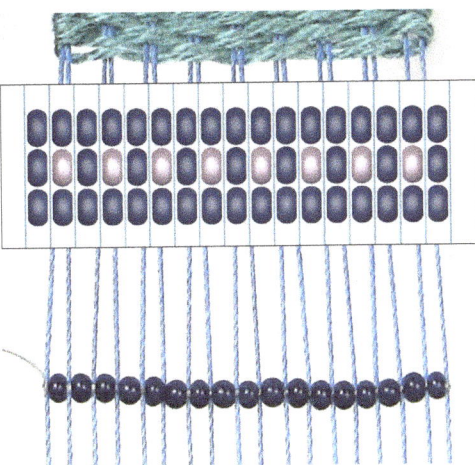

Begin bead section 3 well away from the doubled tencel section because it will be difficult to space the beads between the doubled warps near the tencel. Take care not to pierce the warp threads so this section can be moved directly adjacent to the tencel section. Compress the weave.

Combine one strand of metallic and one strand of tencel to weave the next section in simple over-under weave. Compress the weave. Now rotate the loom and repeat these sections on the other end so there is a space in the center of the warp.

Compress the weave. Begin the striped beaded section with one full row of dark blue beads, then alternate dark blue and silver-lined aqua. End at the opposite side with one full row of dark blue, crammed in so the warp is as compressed as possible. Depending on your size, this alternating section may vary in relative length from what is shown in the photo. Excess nylon thread tails over 5" long can be used to attached 8°s in the next section; secure and trim shorter thread tails.

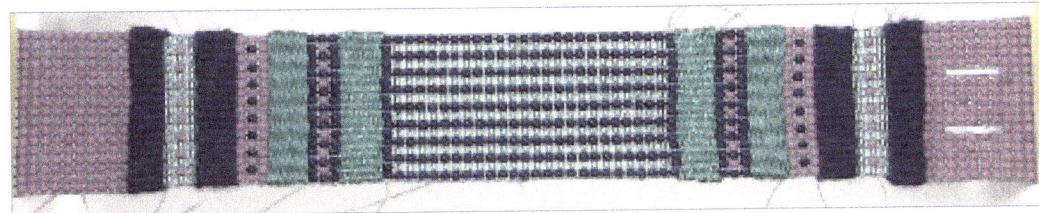

Add the decorative 8°s to the edges. All 8°s are anchored with one 15° 1634F. Place one in the center of each three-row beaded section, with the thread emerging and re-entering in the same outer bead. On the alternating section, place one 8o spanning two outer edge beads. If you have an odd number of rows, don't worry, you won't notice the slight gap at one end when the bracelet is removed from the loom and decompressed slightly.

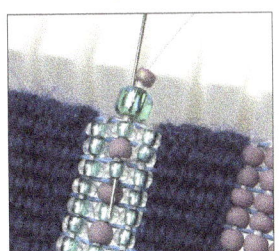

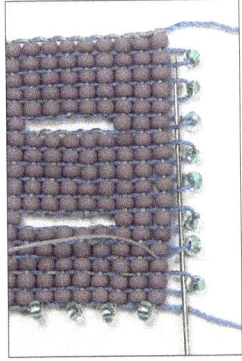
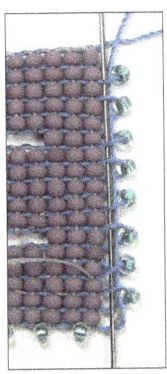

Remove the weave from the loom. Decompress from the center of the bracelet outward until the loops disappear. On the side with tails, remove from the prongs, but before decompressing, run the tails through the loops in both directions. Trim at the outer edges; dab the cut ends with a spot of glue. Decompress all so the weave is as evenly spaced as possible.

Bead patterns

These small repeating patterns can easily be incorporated into your weaves. Examples are shown (at right) in both 11° seed bead and size 11 cylinder bead shapes. Because of their different relative proportions (shown accurately relative to each other at right) squarish cylinder beads will give a more "charted" aspect appearance than seed beads, which are quite oval in shape. Sections of seed beads will appear more elongated than cylinder beads. The two examples are identical in the number of beads and rows, though the seed bead rendering is significantly longer than the cylinder bead rendering due to different shapes.

CYLINDER BEADS ASPECT EXAMPLE

SEED BEADS ASPECT EXAMPLE

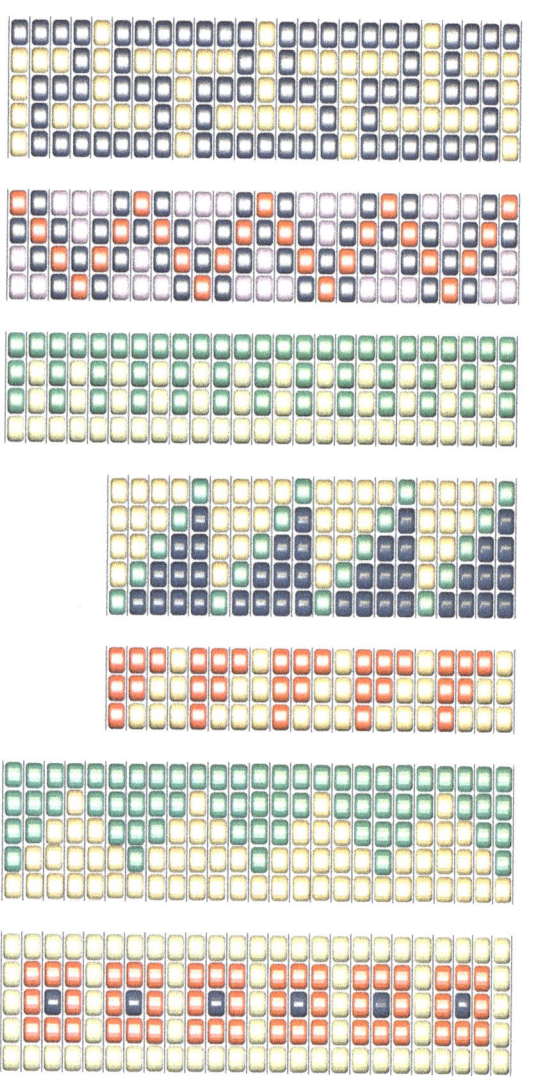

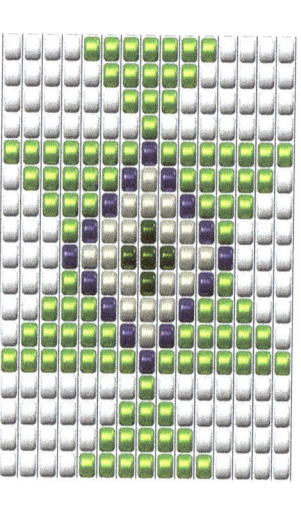

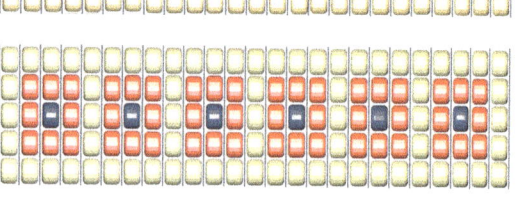

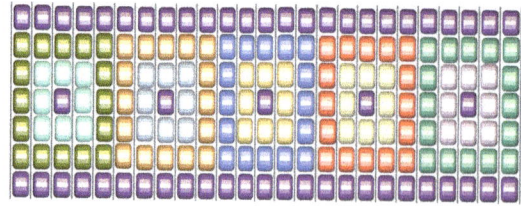

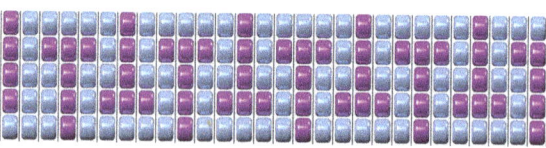

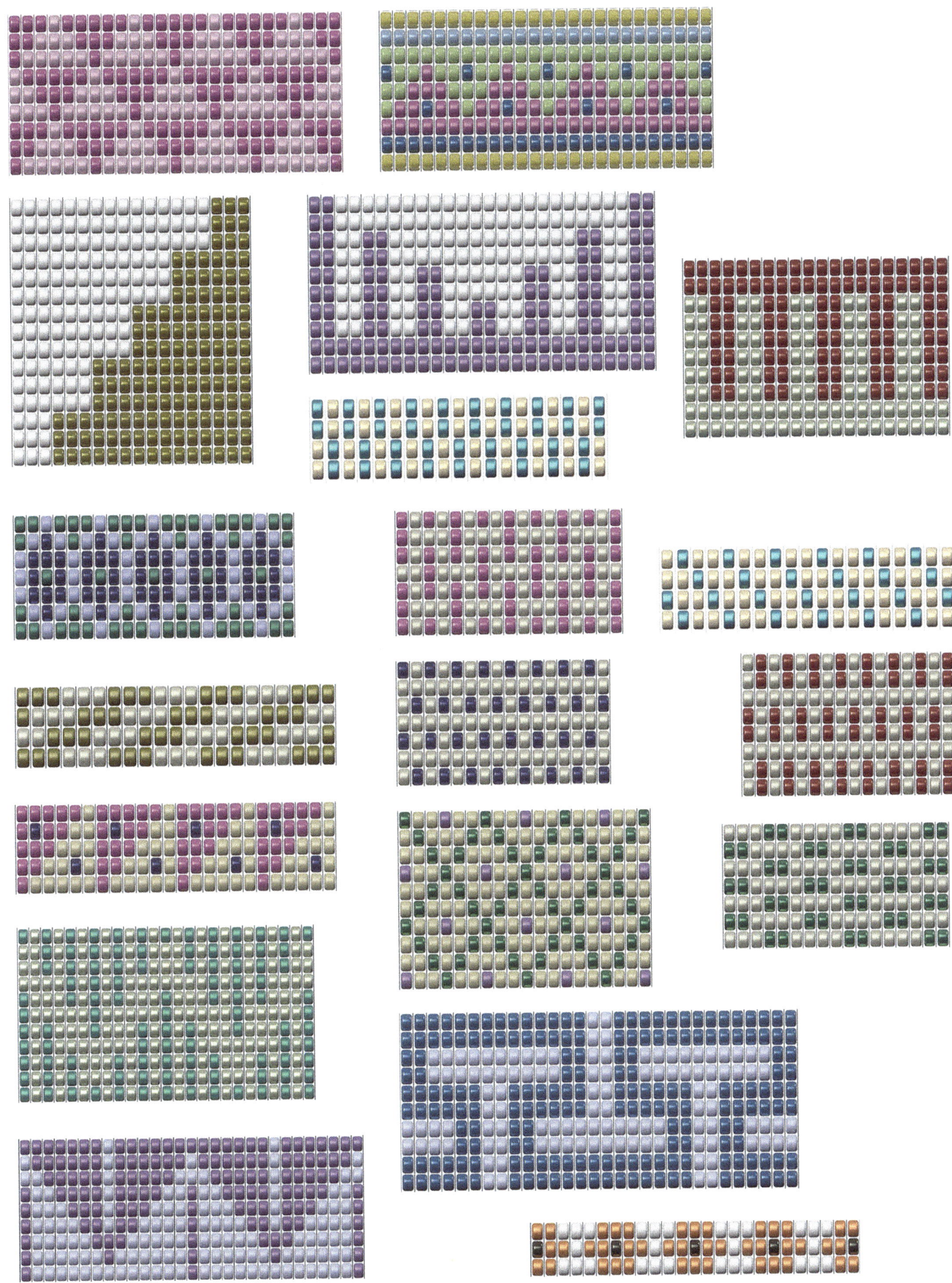

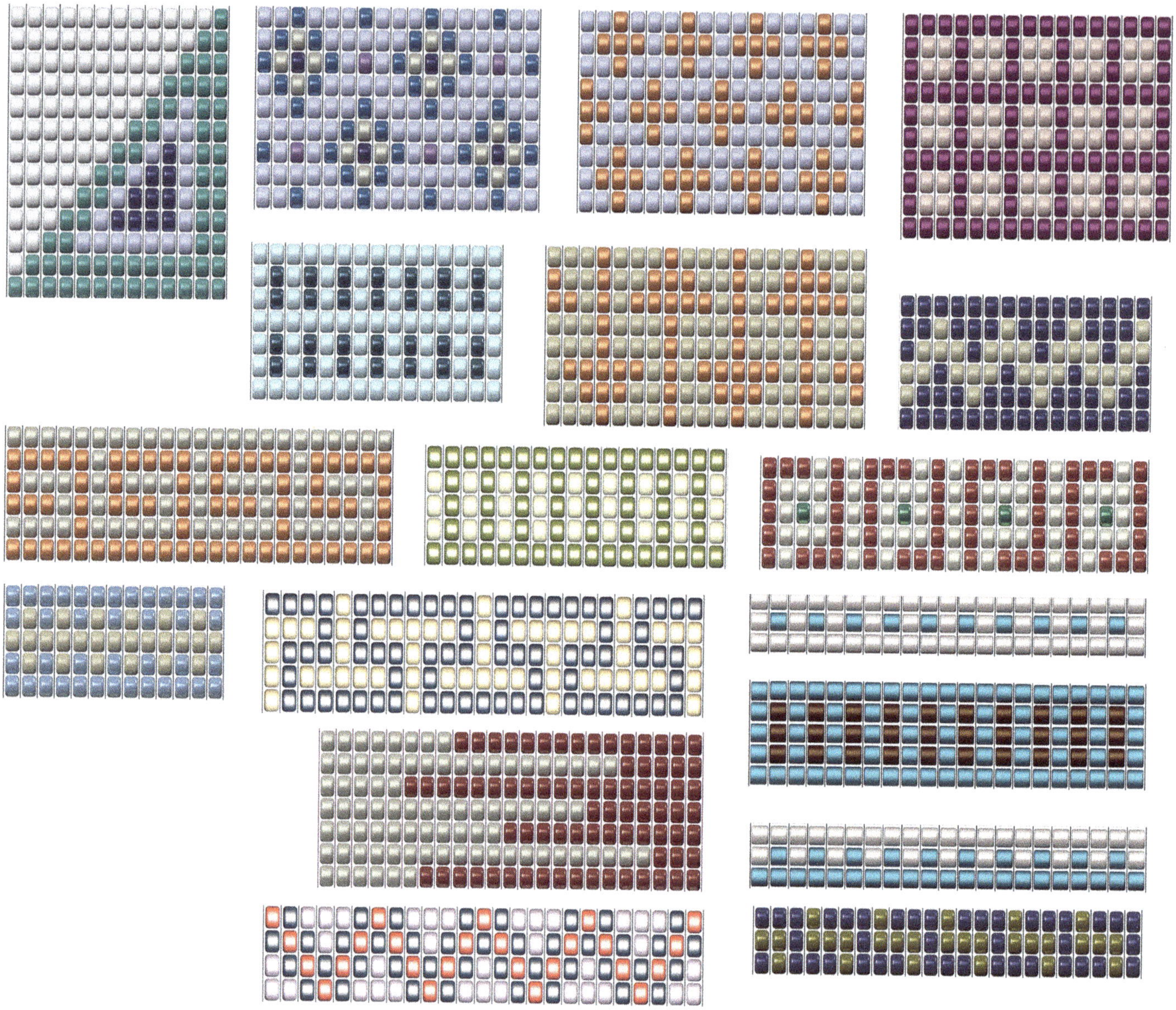

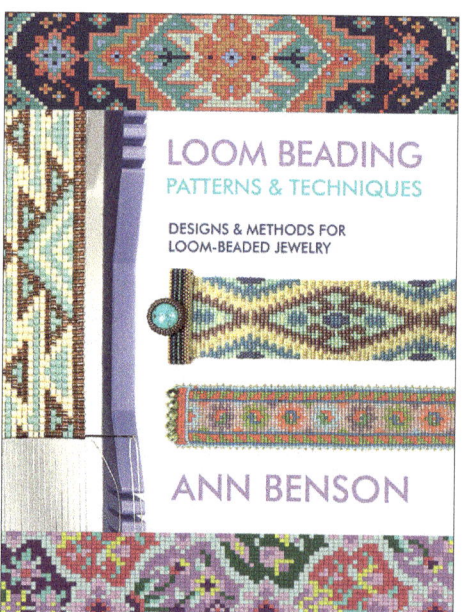

For many more weavable bead patterns, my *Loom Beading* book includes dozens upon dozens of beadable charted patterns that you can incorporate into your bead and fiber weaving designs.

You can use full designs from this book by substituting fibers for some of the beads, or use fractional sections of designs in conjunction with your fiber areas.

BASIC PEYOTE STITCH IN THE ROUND

Peyote stitch in the round starts with an initial ring of beads. Your specific directions will tell you how many beads should be threaded. Create the ring by running the thread back through several beads. This ring will later become the first TWO rounds of stitching.

Pick up one bead, skip one bead on the initial ring. Run the thread through the next bead on the ring. As you tighten the thread the beads shift their positions and form a "zipper tooth" pattern.

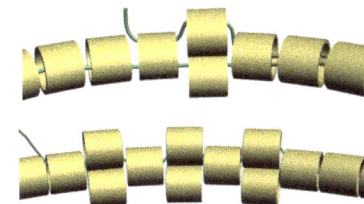

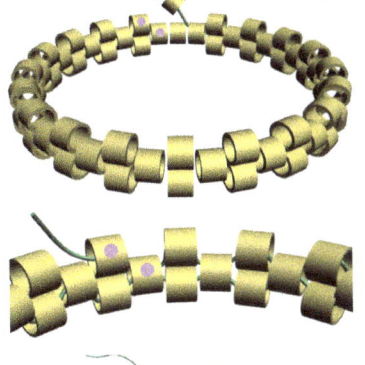

At the end of each round, prior to starting the new round, you must "step up". When you have three beads left on the initial ring and your thread emerges from the first of those beads, you're ready to step up. After picking up the bead to be added, go through TWO beads on the upward diagonal. These beads are shown here dotted in orchid. When you tighten the thread, your three-round ring will have no visible start or end.

Continue in this manner, adding rounds as your directions specify, stepping up in preparation for each new round.

In subsequent rounds, you'll recognize the step up by the distinctive V-shaped gap at the end of the round. Again, you'll pick up your bead and go through TWO beads on the upward diagonal (shown in orchid).

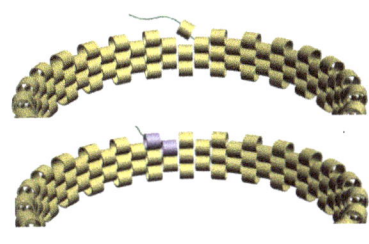

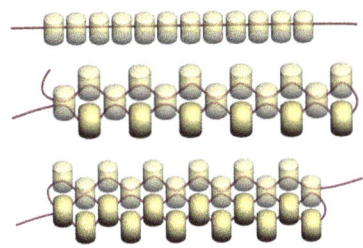

BASIC FLAT PEYOTE STITCH

Flat peyote stitch starts with an initial threading of an even number of beads. This threading will become the first TWO rows as the next row is added. When the initial threading is correct, pick up the first bead of the third row. Skip one bead and run through the next. Continue across the row, skipping every other bead. A zipper pattern will emerge. Do not allow the weave to twist. At the end of each row, reverse direction to start the next row. Add and end threads by weaving invisibly into the existing peyote stitch.

BASIC BEADED EDGING

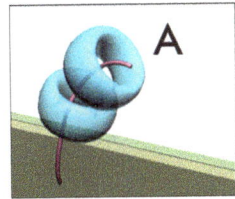
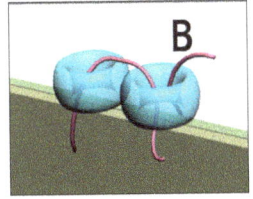
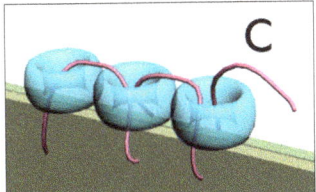
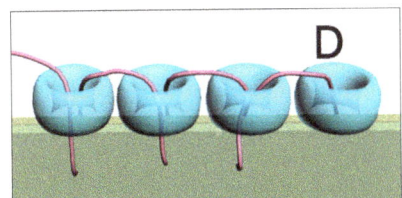

Bring a thread out about 1/16" from the edge; pick up two beads (A). Run through the edge again about two beads' width away, then run through the second bead from inside to outside. Take the slack out of the thread (B). Pick up another bead and run through the edge one bead's width away, then run through this added bead from inside to outside; take the slack out of the thread (C). Diagram D shows a back view of the edging start with four beads in place; the first bead does not have a thread on the back side; it will be added later when you connect the last and first beads.

SQUARE STITCH

Start by threading on the number of beads in the desired width. Pick up another bead and loop it into the last bead of your initial threading. Run through the added bead and pick up another bead. Loop backward through the adjacent bead in the initial threading, then forward through the newly added bead. Continue in the manner until the required number of beads have been added in the row.

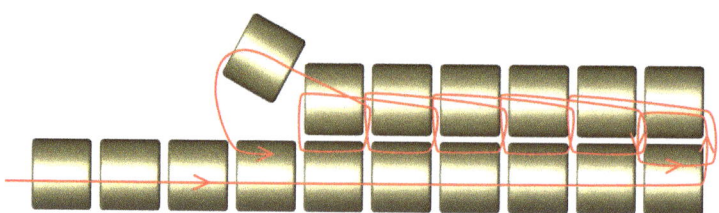

Contacting the author

By email: annbensonbeading@gmail.com
Through Etsy: message through Ann Benson Beading on Etsy
By mail: Ann Benson Frost, 5461 Canna Ct., Port Orange FL 32128
Through Instagram: annbensonbeading

Sourcing

Visit the sourcing page on annbensonbeading.com for the most updated sourcing information. Sources listed on this page have been used by me with satisfactory results.

On-line sourcing through search engines will yield amazing results. Be specific in your search terms; you will refine your results if you include sizes, colors, and finishes when you're sure of what you're seeking.

Software used

- Adobe PhotoShop
- Adobe Illustrator
- Adobe InDesign
- Adobe Bridge
- Adobe Premiere
- MacBook Finder
- Cinema 4D Animation Software
- iCloud

Permissions

What you CAN do with the material in this book:
- All personal non-commercial uses are permitted
- Sell stitched pieces created from material in this book with design attribution to the author
- Teach classes using material from this book with prior permission from the author
- Post photos of your creations from this book with design attribution to the author

What you CANNOT do with the material in this book:
- Reproduce any designs or instructional material from this book for resale
- Use any material in this book as part of a kit excepting author-permitted instructional use
- Teach classes using material from this book without prior permission from the author

Also from **Ann Benson**:

Available at etsy.com/shop/annbensonbeading

Available on Amazon

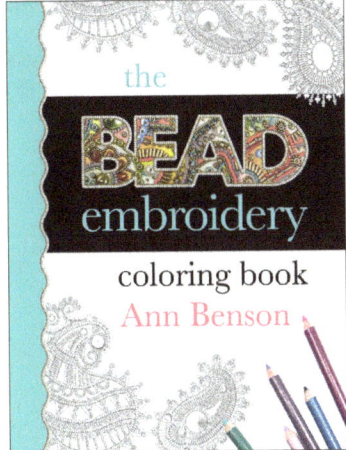
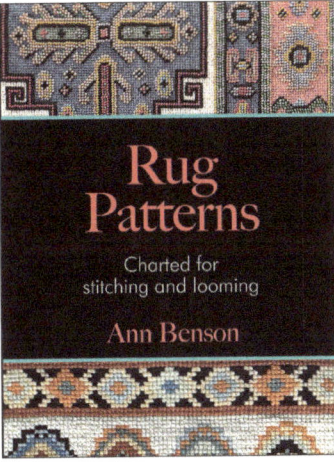
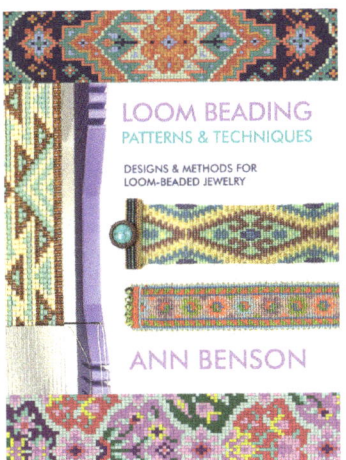

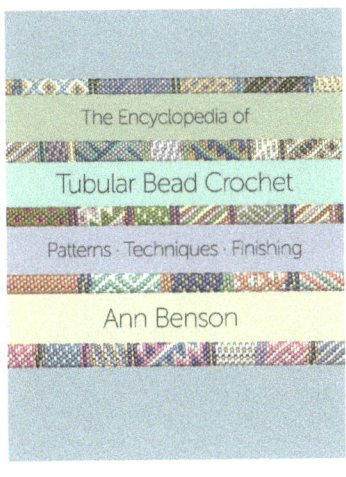
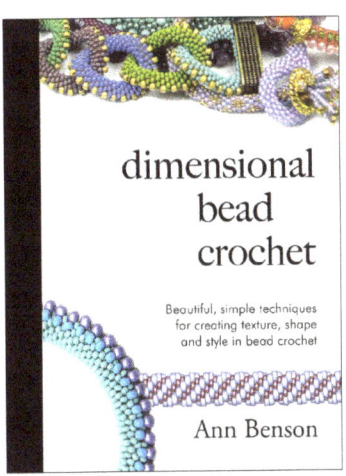
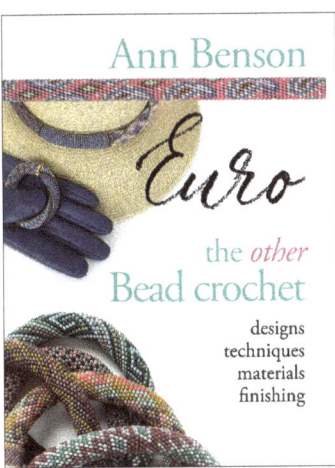

About the author

Ann Benson is an American master bead and needle artist whose body of work includes hundreds of patterns, books and tutorials. She is a YouTube instructional influencer with millions of views and myriad followers. Ann holds a certification in graphic design from Rhode Island School of Design and is renowned for the clarity and thoroughness of her crafting instructions.

Ann is also the author of The Plague Trilogy historical novels (Random House) including *The Plague Tales, The Burning Road*, and *The Physician's Tale*. Ann's latest novel Ambrosia is published under her own imprint.

Ann divides her time between homes in Florida and Cape Cod, where she and husband Gary Frost enjoy their children, grandchildren and friends.

Indexes

Techniques

Designs

www.ingramcontent.com/pod-product-compliance
Lightning Source LLC
Chambersburg PA
CBHW041119120626
46547CB00019B/2768